Routledge Revivals

The English Charlemagne Romances

The English Charlemagne Romances

Part VI. The Taill of Rauf Coilyear (about 1475 A.D.) (from the unique copy of Lekpreuik's edition of 1572) with fragments of Roland and Vernagu and Otuel (from the unique auchinleck MS., about 1330 A.D.)

Sidney, J. H. Herrtage

Routledge
Taylor & Francis Group

First published by N. Trübner & CO.

This edition first published in 2018 by Routledge
2 Park Square, Milton Park, Abingdon, Oxon, OX14 4RN
and by Routledge
711 Third Avenue, New York, NY 10017

Routledge is an imprint of the Taylor & Francis Group, an informa business

© Taylor & Francis

Publisher's Note
The publisher has gone to great lengths to ensure the quality of this reprint but points out that some imperfections in the original copies may be apparent.

Disclaimer
The publisher has made every effort to trace copyright holders and welcomes correspondence from those they have been unable to contact.

A Library of Congress record exists under ISBN: 12017830

ISBN 13: 978-1-138-60485-8 (hbk)
ISBN 13: 978-1-138-60486-5 (pbk)
ISBN 13: 978-0-429-46275-7 (ebk)

The Taill of Rauf Coilyear

WITH THE FRAGMENTS OF

Roland and Vernagu

AND

Otuel.

Early English Text Society

Extra Series. No. XXXIX.

1882.

BERLIN :   ASHER & CO., 53 MOHRENSTRASSE.
NEW YORK: C. SCRIBNER & CO.; LEYPOLDT & HOLT.
PHILADELPHIA : J. B. LIPPINCOTT & CO.

THE
ENGLISH CHARLEMAGNE ROMANCES.

PART VI.

The Taill of Rauf Coilyear

(ABOUT 1475 A.D.)

(FROM THE UNIQUE COPY OF LEKPREUIK'S EDITION OF 1572)

WITH THE FRAGMENTS OF

Roland and Vernagu

AND

Otuel

(FROM THE UNIQUE AUCHINLECK MS., ABOUT 1330 A.D.)

RE-EDITED FROM THE ORIGINALS,

with Introduction, Notes, and Glossary,

BY

SIDNEY J. H. HERRTAGE, B.A.,

EDITOR OF "SIR FERUMBRAS," "THE SEGE OFF MELAYNE," "THE LYF OF
CHARLES THE GRETE," THE "CATHOLICON ANGLICUM," ETC.

LONDON:

PUBLISHED FOR THE EARLY ENGLISH TEXT SOCIETY,

BY N. TRÜBNER & CO., 57 & 59, LUDGATE HILL.

MDCCCLXXXII.

Extra Series.

XXXIX.

———

BUNGAY: CLAY AND TAYLOR, THE CHAUCER PRESS.

INTRODUCTION.

Rauf Coilȝear, p. v.　　　　*Roland and Vernagu*, p. vii, xiv.
Otuel, p. vii, xiii, xv.

THE present part of the Early English Text Society's series of
Charlemagne Romances contains three pieces, all unique, and all only
once before printed. The first piece, "The Taill of Rauf Coilȝear,"
is here reprinted from the only known copy existing, which was discovered in the Advocate's Library in Edinburgh in 1821. Nothing
whatever is known of the author of the poem. He certainly lived
before 1500, for Dunbar, in his address to the king, refers to the
"taill" as follows :—

> "Quhen servit is all uder man,
> Gentiil and semple off every clan,
> Kyne of *Rauf Colyard* and Johne the Reif,
> Nathing I get, na conqueis can,
> Excess of thought dois one mischeif."

And Douglas, in his "Palice of Honour," written in the year 1501,
also couples Rauf Coilȝear and John the Reeve—

> "I saw *Raf Colyear* with hes thrawin brow,
> Craibit Johne the Reif, and auld Cowkelpis Low."

The copy in the Advocate's Library was, as will be seen from the
colophon, printed in 1572 at St. Andrews, by Robert Lekpreuik.
The "taill" begins on leaf A ij, and occupies fourteen pages. The
subject is one which appears to have been a favourite one in all
ages. The idea of a king disguising himself, in order to mix freely
amongst his subjects without being recognized, whatever his motive,
has frequently recommended itself to English ballad-makers. Thus
we have the ballads of "The King and the Miller of Mansfield,"
"King Henry and the Soldier," "King James I. and the Tinker,"
"King William III. and the Forester," "King Alfred and the Shep-
herd," "King Edward IV. and the Tanner," "King Henry VIII. and
the Cobbler," and the oldest of all, "John de Reeue," or "John the

Reeve," a ballad written in the opinion of Prof. Hales about the middle of the 15th century, but, according to Mr. Wright, in the latter part of the 14th century. It was certainly written after 1377 and before 1461.[1]

The fact that Charles the Great and his "Duchepeiris" are introduced into the poem, and that the scene is laid partly on a wild moor near Paris, and partly in Paris itself, would lead to the conclusion that it had a French origin; but there are, probably, no real grounds for such a conclusion. The number of French idioms is far fewer than we should expect to find in a translation or adaptation; those which do occur, *e. g. pardie, in fay, bone fay*, are nearly all colloquial, and such as, from the intercourse between the two countries, might well be familiar to a native of Scotland.

The poem, as pointed out by Dr. Irving,[2] begins in a similar manner to the "Awnturs of Arthur."[3] Both are written in 13-line alliterative stanzas, the only difference being in the scheme of rimes, which in the "Awnturs" is *abababababaccca*, and in "Rauf Coilȝear," *abababababcdddc*. For this reason Dr. Irving conjectured that possibly the two poems are by the same hand. In all probability the poem is quite original, the reference to an authority, "as the buik sayis," l. 355, being nothing more than one of those phrases which the authors of romances so frequently inserted in order to give a fictitious air of authenticity to their compositions.[4] Whoever the author was, he deserves credit for the really quaint humour with which he has worked out his subject. It is impossible to say exactly when the poem was first written, since "the whole orthography has been assimilated to that of the 16th century," and in its present shape belongs to what Dr. Murray defines as the "Middle Period" of

---

[1] It is reprinted in full by Prof. Hales and Mr. Furnivall in "Bishop Percy's Folio MS." 1868, vol. ii. pp. 550—594. My own belief is that it was written not later than 1400. I do not think the use of such a construction as "thou had wedded Iohn daughter reeue," that is, the daughter of John the Reeve, came down so late as 1450; though common in the 14th century. See examples in note to p. 41, l. 154, below.

[2] "History of Scottish Poetry," ed. J. A. Carlyle, M.D. Edinburgh, 1861, pp. 88—93.

[3] Printed for the Camden Society in "Three Metrical Romances," pp. 1—36.

[4] See Dr. Hausknecht's note to the 'Sowdone of Babylone,' l. 26. But in this case it may mean that the service was done as the book directs.

Lowland Scotch.[1] Probably we shall not be far wrong in assigning it to the middle of the second half of the 15th century.

The description of the deadly duel between Rauf and the Saracen is a really comical burlesque of the combats described in Sir Ferumbras, Otuel, &c., and we may be pardoned for entertaining a slight suspicion that the promise of the hand of Joanna in the one case, and of Belesent in the other, had probably more to do with the conversions of the Saracens than either the arguments of Roland, or the descent of the dove on the head of Otuel.

The second and third poems contained in the present part are printed from the celebrated Auchinleck MS. They were printed, but far from correctly, for the Abbotsford Club in 1836, together with a fragment of a romance of Alexander, contained in the same MS.[2] In both, the first letter is always separated from the second by a pretty wide interval. Both are unfortunately defective, having been mutilated for the sake of the illuminations which have been torn out. " Rouland and Vernagu " has not, however, suffered much : the loss at the beginning probably only amounting to eight lines. "Otuel" has fared worse, having lost eight lines near the beginning, and probably a leaf at the end. The two poems were analyzed by Ellis, the first under the title of " Roland and Ferragus," the second under that of " Sir Otuel."[3] Of the latter, he says that " a second MS., in six-lined stanzas, is in the possession of W. Fillingham, Esq. The style of this is much more languid and feeble, resembling pretty nearly the diction of the romance which we have just examined [" Roland and Ferragus "]. It has, however, the merit of completing the story, and of furnishing a paraphrase of Turpin's Chronicle from the period of the death of Ferragus to the battle of Roncesvalles." This MS. has been lost sight of, and I have not been able to gain any information as to its whereabouts. I therefore here reprint Ellis's analysis of that part of it which forms the continuation to " Otuel."

[1] " Dialect of the Southern Counties of Scotland," 1873, p. 57.

[2] " Ancient Metrical Romances," from the Auchinlech MS. Edinburgh, 1836, pp. i—xxvii, 84.

[3] " Specimens of Early English Metrical Romance," 1805, vol. III. pp. 283—355.

" In the continuation of the story, Otuel appears to be almost forgotten, though his name occurs two or three times towards the end of the romance, for the sole purpose, as it should seem, of justifying its title. I have already observed that such a continuation would scarcely deserve notice, but that it presents us with the concluding scene in Turpin's history, the battle of Roncesvalles.

Charles, having thus terminated the campaign of Lombardy, led his unsuccessful rival to Paris, where Garsie, convinced that it was out of the power of Mahomet or Apolyn to obtain for him such terms as he might secure by embracing Christianity, consented to be baptized by the hands of archbishop Turpin. Soon after this, Charles received intelligence that Ibrahim king of Seville, having united his forces with those of the king of Cordes, was encamped near that city ; he therefore collected an army with all possible expedition, and marched to attack them. He found them

> ' With batayles stern ten ;
> The first waren foot-men
>   That grisliche were of cheer ;
> With hair they were be-hong,
> And beardys swithe long,
>   And hornes in hond bare.'

These ugly troops were also provided with numberless bells and other sonorous instruments, which, added to the hideous shouts and yells with which they advanced to the attack, produced a discord truly diabolical. It will readily be believed that the valorous knights, who formed the van of the Christian army, were very little disturbed either by the abominable features, or by the grotesque gesticulations, or by the dissonant noises of these uncouth antagonists : but their horses, who were perfectly unprepared for an encounter with such musicians in masquerade, utterly refused to approach them, and, when roused by the spur from the lethargy of astonishment into which they had been plunged by the unexpected sight, suddenly dispersed in all directions, and, charging the French infantry with the rapidity of lightning, threw them into confusion ; after which, communicating the panic to the body of reserve, they hurried the astonished Charlemagne, together with his twelve peers, several miles from the field of battle.

The infantry, having at length gained a commanding eminence, were easily rallied, because they could not run much further ; but it was not till late in the evening that they were joined by the cavalry, when the king commanded them to pitch their tents. On the following morning he gave orders that the ears of all the horses in the army should be carefully stopped with wax, and that they should at the same time be hood-winked ; after which he marched forward in good order to meet the enemy. The Saracens were now repulsed in their turn ; but maintained an obstinate conflict in defence of their sacred standard, which was carried in a car drawn by twelve oxen. On this occasion, Charlemagne exhibited the greatest heroism, and, drawing his good sword Joyeuse, rushed into the midst of his enemies, forced his way to the standard, cut in two the long and massive spear on which it was reared, and shortly after clove the skull of the ferocious Ibrahim, the tyrant of Seville. Eight thousand Saracens fell in this battle; and on the following day the king of Cordes, who had escaped into the city, was forced to surrender, and to do homage to Charles, after promising to renounce his former creed, and to embrace the doctrines of Christianity.

Immediately after this victory, the French army was called off to repress the inroads of the king of Navarre; and on this occasion the pious Charles was gratified by a fresh miracle. It is well known that those who die in battle against the infidels are rewarded by the crown of martyrdom; and if this were not a matter of course, it was in the present case secured by the express promise made by St. James to Charles in his sleep. Now the good king wished to know how many of his knights were predestined to lose their lives on this occasion, and prayed to heaven that his curiosity might be satisfied. Accordingly, the intended victims were all marked with a red cross on their shoulder; but Charles, finding their number much greater than he expected, and wishing to obtain a cheaper victory, left them all behind in a place of security, attacked the enemy, gained the battle, and returned without loss. In the mean time those for whom he was thus solicitous had all expired; and thus did the good king learn that it is useless to oppose the designs of Providence.

Having at length secured the submission of Spain, by distributing all his conquests, either amongst his own friends or amongst those of his benefactor St. James, Charlemagne became desirous of returning into France; but feeling some uneasiness at leaving behind him two Saracen kings, named Marsire and Baligand, who then resided at Saragossa, he despatched an ambassador to inform them that they must immediately consent to be baptized, or else pay him tribute. The ambassador whom he chose for this mission was the celebrated Guines or Ganelon, whose duty to his sovereign and to his country was soon overpowered by a present of thirty *somers* (beasts of burthen) laden with gold and silver, which the artful Saracens offered to him on condition of his undertaking to lead the French army into the defiles of the forest of Roncesvalles.

> And thritti steedes with gold fine,
> To Charles sent that Sarrazin,
>   All they were white as flour;
> And an hundred tuns of wine,
> That was both good and fine,
>   And swithe fair coloùr.[1]

[1] Gaguin, in his translation of Turpin, adds to this present a thousand beautiful damsels, " pour en faire à leur voulenté," and further explains to us

At the same time they permitted Ganelon to make, in their name, whatever promises he might think necessary for the purpose of preventing any suspicions in the mind of Charlemagne.

The traitor executed his commission with great address, and suggested such a disposition of the French army as insured the destruction of Roland and of all his companions. Charles in person commanded one half of the army, and was suffered to pass the mountains unmolested, and to descend into the open country ; but no sooner had Roland, who conducted the second division, advanced into the forest of Roncesvalles, than he found himself attacked on all sides by the Saracens, who had been previously posted on every eminence, and had concerted every measure for the surprise of the Christians. Roland, as might be expected, made a desperate resistance, and, being assisted by all the best knights of France, nearly annihilated the first body of his assailants ; but the Saracens continued to receive constant reinforcements, while the Christians were exhausted by fatigue and hunger. Constantine of Rome, Ogier le Danois, Reynald de Montauban, Sir Bertram the standard-bearer, and many others of less note, after performing prodigies of valour, were successively slain. Olivier, covered with wounds, was at length overpowered, and Roland, after singly cutting his way through the enemy, perceived that all hopes of retreat were lost, and that nothing remained for him but to seek for an opportunity of dying honourably in the field.

After wandering for some time in the forest, he discovered a single Saracen, whom he secured and bound to a tree ; after which having gained an eminence from whence he could discover the situation of the enemy, he sounded his ivory horn, collected round him a small number of his fugitive soldiers, and, returning with them to his prisoner, unbound him, and promised him life on condition that he should point out to them the person of king Marsire. The Saracen readily obeyed, and showed him the king mounted on a bay charger, and bearing a golden dragon on his shield ; upon which Roland, setting spurs to his horse, dashed through the surrounding guards, and with one blow clove his enemy to the saddle-bows. Baligand collected the remains of the Saracen army, and retreated to Saragossa.

Roland, now covered with wounds, and beginning to suffer severely from fever and from thirst, dismounted from his horse, lay down under a tree, and, drawing his good sword Durindale,

> ' Tho he began to make his moan,
> And fast looked thereupon,
> As he it held in his hond.

---

the real cause of the terrible disaster which befel the Christians. " Mais pour autant que les gens de l'ost s'estoient enyvrés, les nuits précédentes, du vin des Sarrazins que Ganelon avoit amené, aucuns avoient commis le peché de fornication avec las femmes Sarrazines, et aultres femmes chretiennes de France." Cap. 20.

> " O sword of great might,
> " Better bare never no knight,
>   " To win with no loud !
> " Thou hast y-be in many batayle,
> " That never Sarrazin, sauns fayle,
>   " Ne might thy stroke withstond.
> " Go ! let never no Paynim
> " Into batayle bear him,
>   " After the death of Roland !
> " O sword of great powere,
> " In this world n' is nought thy peer,
> " Of no metal y-wrought ;
> " All Spain and Galice
> " Through grace of God and thee, y-wis,
>   " To Christendom ben brought.
> " Thou art good withouten blame ;
> " In thee is graven the holy name
>   " That all things made of nought ! " '

After these words he rose, and, exerting his whole force, struck the sword against a rock in hopes of breaking it : but Durindale sunk deep into the solid stone ; and when he had with some difficulty drawn it out, he found the edge uninjured.

The dying hero now blew his ivory horn, in hopes of drawing round him some friends, if any such had escaped from the battle, to whom he might consign his sword, and who might join with him in prayer during his last moments. No one appeared. He made a second effort, and with such violence that he burst the horn, and at the same time so distended all his veins that his wounds began to bleed most abundantly, and soon reduced him almost to extremity. The sound of this blast was distinctly heard in the army of Charlemagne, who wished to return in search of his nephew, but was persuaded by Ganelon, that Roland could be in no danger, but was most probably amusing himself by hunting in the forest. It brought, however, to Roland, two of his companions, Sir Baldwin and Sir Terry, who having escaped the general slaughter, had been hitherto wandering through the forest, and whom he sent in search of some water ; which, however, they were unable to find. In the mean time a Saracen, coming by chance to the spot where the hero lay, endeavoured to carry off Durindale ; but Roland, suddenly starting up, wrenched the sword from his hand, killed him with one blow, and fainted with the exertion : so that Sir Baldwin, finding him apparently lifeless, laid him with great care across his horse, took care of his sword and horn, and conducted him to an adjoining valley, where the hero, recovering his senses, had time to make a very long prayer before he expired ; when his soul was immediately carried up to heaven by a troop of angels.

Archbishop Turpin was, at this moment, saying mass for the souls of the dead, and distinctly heard the songs of these angels, who were, however, too distant to be seen : but at the same time he discovered

and interrogated a troop of black fiends, who were flying to hell with
the soul of king Marsire, and who reported to him the death of
Roland, which he instantly notified to Charlemagne.

The good king instantly set off towards Roncesvalles, and being
met by Sir Baldwin, who confirmed the deposition of the devils, was
conducted by him to the body of Roland, over which he swooned two
or three times, and uttered many learned but tedious lamentations.[1]
He then prepared for vengeance ; and, having first prayed to Heaven
that the sun might be stopped for him, as it had formerly been for
Josua (a favour which was readily granted to him), led his army
against Saragossa, where Baligand had found a retreat. In this battle,
Sir Turpin distinguished himself by many acts of extraordinary
valour, as did also Sir Hugon, Sir Thibaut, Charlemagne, and Otuel,
of whom we have long lost sight, but who is now brought forward
for the purpose of killing Perigon, king of Persia, whilst Turpin has
the honour of destroying the treacherous Baligand. Sixty thousand
Saracens, it seems, were slain in this long and murderous day ; after
which Charles returned to the fatal field of Roncesvalles ; where Sir
Terry, having formally accused Ganelon of causing the destruction of
the French army, and having proved his charge in single combat, that
traitor was condemned to be hanged, and then torn into quarters by
four horses. Having thus revenged the death of his nephew,

> ' Charlys took his knights,
> And went to Roland, anon rights,
>   With swithe great dolour ;
> Rolandys body he let dight,
> With myrrh and balm anon right,
>   With swithe good odour.'

"Rouland and Vernagu" can claim credit for little more than
being a fair translation or adaptation of the Chronicle of the pseudo-
Turpin, as will be seen from a comparison with the Latin version, of
which I reprint the chapter containing the account of the duel of
Roland and Vernagu, or Ferragus. In l. 328 the translator expressly
refers to his Latin original, and in l. 481 he evidently assumes it to
have been written by Turpin himself.

---

[1] Though these lamentations are insufferable in the drawling stanzas of our
English translator, they are not unentertaining in the old French of Gaguin.
" O le bras dextre de mon corps ! l'honneur des Gaules ! l'espée de chevalerie !
Hache inflexible, haubergeon incorruptible et heaulme du salut ! Comparé à
Judas Machabeus par ta valeur et prouesse, ressemblant à Sanson, et pareil à
Jonatas fils de Saul par la fortune de ta triste mort ! O chevalier très aspre et
bien enseigné à combattre ! fort plus fort, et très fort ! génie royal ! destruc-
teur des Sarrazins ! des bons Chrestiens défenseur ! le mur et deffence des
eleves ! le ferme baston des orphelins et veuves ! la viande et réfection des
pauvres ! la révélation des églises ! langue sans avoir menti ès jugemens de
toutes choses," &c. (chap. xxiv.). (See *Charles the Grete*, pp. 240-1.)

"Otuel," on the other hand, is written with a considerable amount of spirit and animation. It is connected with "Rouland and Vernagu" by the concluding lines of the latter, the "Sege of Melayne" coming in as an interlude between the two. It differs in so many respects from "Roland and Otuell" that the relations of the two may be compared to those of the "Sowdone of Babylone" and "Sir Ferumbras." It is, in fact, not a translation so much as an adaptation or reproduction, the author not considering himself confined to a strict following of his text, but free to modify, add, or omit at pleasure. In its opening it agrees with the Middlehill MS. of "Otinel," rather than the Vatican MS., for while the latter gives the time of Otuel's appearance as "à Pasques," the former says: "ço ᵕfu le jor dunt li Innocent sunt." In "Roland and Otuell," l. 193, as in "Otinel," Otuel agrees to surrender his sword to Roland; but in the present version it will be seen that he indignantly refuses. "Roland and Otuell" again omits the passage describing the death of Arapater (Erpater) at the hands of Otuel (see note to l. 1129), which is briefly related in "Otuel," ll. 1111—1122. Nothing is said in "Otuel" about Ogier's reception and treatment by Clarel's mistress, in which "Roland and Otuell" follows closely the account in "Otinel," and both omit his torture by her on hearing of the death of Clarel. The positions of Roland and Oliver in the episode described in st. cxvii of "Roland and Otuell" are reversed in "Otuel," ll. 1399—1416. The details of the final general engagement differ very considerably, but "Roland and Otuell" follows "Otinel" more closely than does "Otuel." It appears then, on the whole, that "Roland and Otuell" is a tolerably close translation of a French version of "Otinel," which was not, however, identical with the "Otinel," edited by MM. Guessard and Michelant, while "Otuel" is a free adaptation or reproduction of another version, differing in some minor details, but how far it is impossible to say, owing to the loose open manner in which the author of the English poem has treated his subject. In l. 706 he refers to "romaunse" as his authority, but this may be simply for the purpose of gaining credit for his work.

The following are the principal dialectal peculiarities of "Roland and Vernagu" and "Otuel."

In the former the pronouns are—

	S.				P.	
	1	2	3	1	2	3
N	I y ich.	þou.	he hye (116) it.	we.	ȝe.	he (70) þai.
G	mi min.	þi.	his.			her.
D	me.		him.			
A	me.	þe.	him it.		ȝe.	hem.

Ichadel (768) and *ich* (208, 286) = same, very, are noticeable.

The genitives of nouns end in -*es*, except *pin* (396): *winter* (5) is plural as in A.S., and so also *niȝt* (366, 389).

In verbs the infinitive ends in -*en*, but the *n* is generally dropped. We have *resten, gon, ben* (and also *be*), *slen*. Three times we have an ending in -*y* or -*i, answerey* (764), *prechy* (156), *serui* (358): *yse* occurs once (789).

In the present indicative we have one instance, *woni* (166), of an ending in -*i.* In the second person singular we have *comest* (162) and *winnes* (164): the ending in the third person singular is -*th*, and with one exception, *don* (202), the same ending is used throughout in the plural.

Bit for *biddeth* occurs once (56), and we have instances of the coalescence of the first personal pronoun with the verbs, *ichot* (767), *ichil* (2, 430), and *ichaue* (396, 732); the second personal pronoun is frequently attached to the verb, as *hadestow* (514), *astow* (781). In the preterite the plural ending is -*en*, but the *n* is generally omitted.

The plural imperative ends in -*eþ*. Only one present participle occurs, *slepeand* (623).

In the past participles the ending of weak verbs is *t*, of the strong verbs -*en*, but the *n* is sometimes omitted. The prefix *i*- or *y*- (A.S. *ge*) is generally used: thus we have *y-meten, y-schapen, y-sen, y-bore,* and *y-born, y-founde, y-corn, y-herd : forlore* and *forlorn* also occur.

Of inflections of the article we have one instance, "*þan* þridde day" (691), which survived perhaps as a kind of formula: "*þe* nende" occurs in l. 389, and "*þe neue*" in l. 581.

In "Otuel" the following forms occur in the pronouns :—

	S.			P.	
1	2	3	1	2	3
N i, ich, ihc.	þou, þou.	He, ho (1097), ȝo (1001).	we.	ȝe.	þei.
G mi, min, myn	þi, þin	his, hise.		ȝoure.	here, hare (1078).
D me.	þe.	him.			ham (918), hem.
A me.	þe, te.	him.	us.	ȝou.	hem, ham (1660).

Hit is used (103, 384) referring to masculine nouns, as in " Sir Ferumbras ": *beie* for *both* occurs once (529).

In verbs the ending of the infinitive is generally *-en*, but the *-n* is at times omitted : thus we have *habben, habbe,* and *hauen,̓ gon* and *go, sene, seen* and *se, slen* and *sle, ben* and *be,* &c.

In̓ the present indicative the second person singular ends in *-est,* but once we have *tou wille :* the third person singular ends in *-eþ.*

In the plural the first and third persons end in *-en,* the *-n* being sometimes omitted.

The second person ends in *-eþ,* except in l. 2, where we have *willen,* and in l. 613, where we have *habben.* The termination is omitted in ll. 614 and 979.

Rit for *rideth, halt* for *holdeth,* and *bytit* for *betideth,* occur once each. There is no instance of this coalescence of the first personal pronoun with the verb, but the second is sometimes found attached on to its verb as *dostou,* and the third in one instance, *taket* (210).

In the preterite the second person singular ends in *-est,* and the third person plural in *-en,* the *n* as usual being frequently omitted.

The plural imperative ends in *-eþ.*

The present participle ends in *-ing* or *-yng,* except in one instance, *fleinde* (1460).

The past participles of the weak verbs end in *-t,* of the strong in *-en,* the *-n* being frequently omitted. The prefix *i-* or *y-* is omitted as often as it is used : thus we have *i-comen, comen,* and *come, i-be* and *ben, y-gon, gon,* and *go* (1012). We find also *lorn, i-loren,* and *lose* (1398).

The following instances of plurals of nouns in *-n* occur : *foon* (64), *honden* (174), *sinnen* (394), *gamen* (710), *steeden* (1007), and *eien* (1100) : *hond* occurs in l. 916.

The verbs *have, will, wist,* and *be* have negative forms : *nist, nult, nold, nas, nelle, nere, nis, nabbe,* &c.

Adverbs in *-iche* occur in ll. 346, 365, 559-60 and 1158, &c.

In ll. 317 and 1528 we have perhaps an instance of the tendency to drop the *t* of the second person of verbs which is frequent in the " Bestiary" and "Genesis and Exodus."   (See Dr. Morris' Introd. to the latter, p. xviii.)

The use of *u* for *i,* as *hul* for hill, *whuche* for which, &c., is not uncommon.

A consideration of these forms and peculiarities leads to the conclusion that the poems were written by an East-Midland scribe, who from some reason or other was acquainted with Southern literature.

With regard to the date of composition of the poems the Auchinleck MS., from which they are here reprinted, is generally ascribed to c. 1330 A. D.; but, were such not the case, so far as " Roland and Vernagu " and " Otuel " are concerned I should feel disposed to assign a somewhat later date.

I am indebted to Dr. Murray for the collation of " Rauf Coilȝear " with the original, and also for numerous hints and suggestions as to the poem, and to Mr. Furnivall for information as to John de Reeue.

Finchley, N.
Christmas, 1882.

APPENDIX.

DE BELLO FERRACUTI GIGANTIS, ET DE OPTIMA DISPUTATIONE ROLANDI.[1]

STATIMVERO nunciatum est Carolo, quod apud Nageram, Gigas nomine Ferracutus, qui fuit de genere Goliad, aduenerat de oris Syriæ, quem cum viginti millibus Turcorum Babylonis Admiraldus ad bellandum Carolum regem miserat. Hic vero lanceam aut sagittam aut spatham non formidabat, vim quadraginta fortium possidebat. Quapropter Carolus ilico Nageram adit. Mox vt eius aduentum Ferracutus agnouit, egressus ab vrbe, singulare certamen, scilicet vnum militem contra alterum, petiit. Tunc mittitur ei primum à Carolo Ogerius Dacus : quem mox vt solum Gigas in campo aspexit, suauiter iuxta illum vadit, et ilico eum brachio dextro cum omnibus suis armis amplexatus est, et deportans illum, cunctis videntibus, in oppidum suum leuiter, quasi esset vna mitissima ouis. Erat enim statura eius quasi cubitis duodecim, et facies eius longa quasi vnius cubiti, et nasus illius vnius palmi mensurati, et brachia et crura eius quatuor cubitorum erant, et digiti ejus tribus palmis. Deinde misit ad eum causa bellandi Carolus Rainaldum de Alba Spina, et gigas detulit illum solo brachio illico in carcerem oppidi sui. Deinde mittitur Constantinus rex Romanus et Oliverius comes,

News having reached Charles that Ferragus, a Saracen giant, was at Nagera challenging any French knight to single combat,

Ogier is first sent against him.

But the Saracen lifts him easily with one hand and carries him off.

Then Rainald is sent, but he too meets with the same fate, as also do Constantine and Oliver, whom

<hr>

[1] De Vita Caroli Magni et Rolandi Historia Joanni Turpino, Archiepiscopo Ramensi vulgo, tributa. Ed. A. Sebastiano Ciampi. Florence, 1822, ch. xviii, pp. 39-49.

et ipsos simul, vnum ad dexteram, et alium ad læuam, in carcerem retrusit. Deinde mittuntur viginti pugnatores, scilicet duo insimul separatim, et illos, similiter carcere mancipauit. His itaque inspectis, Carolus, cunctis insuper admirantibus, neminem postea ausus est mittere ad expugnandum eum. Rolandus tamen vix impetrata licentia à rege, accessit ad Gigantem bellatorem. At ipse Gigas rapuit eum sola manu dextera, et misit eum ante se super equum suum. Cumque illum portaret versus oppidum, Rolandus, resumptis viribus suis, et in Domino confisus arripuit eum per mentum, et statim euertit eum retro super equum, et ceciderunt ambo simul de equo prostrati solo : statimque eleuantur à terra ambo pariter, et ascenderunt equos. Illico Rolandus, spatha propria euaginata, Gigantem occidere putans, equum eius solo ictu per medium trucidauit. Cumque Ferracutus pedes esset, spathamque euaginatam manu tenens ei nimias minas intulisset, Rolandus sua spatha in brachio, quo spatham suam Gigas tenebat, illum percussit, et minimè eum læsit, sed spatham eius é manu excussit. Tunc Ferracutus gladio amisso, percutere putans pugno clauso Rolandum, eius equum in fronte percussit, et læsit, et statim equus obiit. Denique sine gladiis et pedites vsque ad nonam pugnis et lapidibus debellarunt. Die vero aduesperascente impetravit trebas Ferracutus à Rolando vsque in crastinum. Tunc disposuerunt inter se, vt die crastina in bello sine equis et lanceis ambo conuenirent, et concessa pugna ex vtraque parte, vnusquisque ad proprium remeauit hospitium. Crastina vero die, summo diluculo separatim venerunt pedites in campo belli, sicut dispositum fuerat : Ferracutus tamen secum attulit spatham, sed nihil ei valuit, quia Rolandus baculum quemdam retortum et longum[1] secum detulit,

---

[1] Ed. lignum

cum quo tota die illum percussit, et minimè læsit eum.
Percussit et eum cum magnis et rotundis lapidibus, qui
in campo abundantes erant, vsque ad meridiem, illo
sæpe consentiente, sed eum nullo modo lædere potuit.
Tunc impetratis à Rolando trebis, Ferracutus somno
prægrauatus cœpit dormire : Rolandus verò, vt erat
iuuenis alacer, misit lapidem ad caput eius, vt libentius
dormiret.   Nullus enim Christianorum illum tunc occidere audebat, nec ipse Rolandus ; nam talis erat inter eos
institutio, quod si Christianus Saraceno, vel Saracenus
Christiano daret trebam, nullus ei iniuriam faceret ;
et si aliquis trebam datam ante diffidentiam frangeret,
statim interficeretur.   Ferracutus itaque postquam satis
dormiuit euigilauit, et sedit iuxta eum Rolandus, et
cœpit eum interrogare, qualiter ita fortissimus et duris-
simus habebatur, qui avt gladium aut baculum non
formidabat. Per nullum locum Vulnerari, inquit Gigas,
possum nisi per vmbilicum.   Loquebatur ipse lingua
Hispanica, quam Rolandus satis intelligebat.   Tunc
Gigas cœpit Rolandum adspicere et interrogare eum,
dicens : "Tu autem quomodo vocaris?"   "Rolandus,"
inquit, "vocor."   "Cuius generis," inquit Gigas, "es,
qui tam fortiter me expugnas?"   "Francorum genere
oriundus," inquit Rolandus, "sum."   At Ferracutus ait :
"Cuius legis sunt Franci?"   Et Rolandus : "Chris-
tianæ legis Dei gratia sumus, et Christi imperiis
subiacemus, et pro eius fide in quantum possumus,
decertamus."   Tunc paganus audito Christi nomine
ait : "Quis est ille Christus, in quem credis?"   Et
Rolandus, "Filius Dei Patris," inquit, "qui ex virgine
nascitur, cruce patitur, sepulchro sepelitur, et ab inferis
tertia die resuscitatur, et ad Dei Patris dexteram super
cœlos regreditur."   Tunc Ferracutus, "Nos credimus,"
inquit, "quia creator cœli et terræ vnus est Deus, nec
filium habuit nec patrem : scilicet sicut à nullo gener-
atur, ita neminem genuit : Ergo vnus est Deus, non

b 2

Roland attacks
the Saracen with
big stones, but to
no purpose.

At noon Ferragus
is drowsy,
and Roland lets
him have a sleep,
placing a stone
for his pillow.

When he wakes
up Ferragus tells
Roland that he
can be wounded
only in the navel:

and afterwards
asks him his
name and family.

Roland says he is
a Frenchman,
and Ferragus
asks what is the
faith of the
French.

Roland says they
are Christians.

"Who is Christ?"
asks Ferragus.
Roland says,
"The Son of God,
who was born of a
virgin, died on
the cross, and
afterwards
ascended into
heaven."
"But," says
Ferragus, "God is
one, how then can
he be three?"

Roland says, "He is One God in Three Persons."

trinus." "Verum dicis," inquit Rolandus, "quia vnus est : sed cum dicis, Trinus non est, in fide claudicas. Si credis in Patrem, crede et in Filio eius, et in Spiritu sancto. Ipse enim Deus et Pater, Filius, et Spiritus sanctus est, vnus Deus permanens in tribus personis."

"Then," says Ferragus, "there must be three Gods, not one God."

"No," says Roland, "though there are three coeternal and coequal persons in the Trinity, there is but one God.

"Si Patrem," inquit Ferracutus, "dicis esse Deum, Filium Deum, Spiritum sanctum Deum : ergo tres Dii sunt, quod absit, et non vnus Deus." "Nequaquam," inquit Rolandus, "sed vnum Deum et trinum prædico tibi, et vnus est, et trinus est. Totæ tres personæ coæternæ sibi sunt et coæquales. Qualis Pater, talis Filius, talis Spiritus sanctus ; in personis est proprietas, in essentia est vnitas, et in maiestate adoratur æqualitas. Trinum Deum et vnum angeli adorant in cœlis. Et Abraham tres vidit, et vnum adorauit." "Hoc ostende," inquit Gigas, "qualiter tria vnum sint." "Ostendam etiam tibi," inquit Rolandus, " per humanas

As in a harp when played are three things, skill, strings, and the hand, and yet there is but one harp :

and as in the sun are three things, heat, brightness, and whiteness, and yet only one sun,

creaturas : Sicut in cithara, cum sonat, tria sunt, ars scilicet, chordæ, et manus, et vna cithara est ; sic in Deo tria sunt, Pater, et Filius, et Spiritus sanctus, et vnus est Deus. Et sicut in amygdala tria sunt, corium scilicet, nucleus, et testa, et vna tamen amygdala est : sic tres personæ in Deo sunt, et vnus Deus est. In sole tria sunt, candor, splendor, et calor, et tamen vnus sol est. In rota plaustri tria sunt, medium scilicet, brachia, et circulus, et tamen vna rota est. In temetipso tria sunt, corpus scilicet, membra, et anima, et tamen vnus homo es. Sic in Deo et vnitas et trinitas esse per-

so in God are three persons, but one God."
"Now I understand," says Ferragus, "but how could God be born ?"
"As Adam," replies Roland, "was born of none, so the Son of God was born of none, but begotten by God himself."

hibentur." "Nunc," Ferracutus inquit, "trinum Deum et vnum esse intelligo : sed qualiter Pater Filium genuit, ut asseris, ignoro." "Credis," inquit Rolandus. "quod Deus Adam fecit ?" "Credo," inquit Gigas. "Quemadmodum," inquit Rolandus, "Adam à nullo generatus est, tamen filios genuit : sic Deus Pater à nullo generatus est, tamen Filium ineffabiliter ante omnia tempora diuinitus, prout voluit, genuit à semetipso." Et Gigas, "Placent," inquit, "mihi quæ dicis, sed qualiter homo effectus est qui Deus erat, penitus ignoro." "Ille," inquit Rolandus, "qui cœlum et terram et omnia creauit ex nihilo, ipse fecit humanari Filium in virgine sine semine humano, spiramine sacro suo." "In hoc," inquit Gigas, "laboro qualiter sine humano semine, vt asseris, nascitur de virginis vtero." Et Rolandus ait : "Deus qui Adam sine semine alterius formauit, ipse Filium suum sine semine hominis de virgine nasci fecit, et sicut de Deo Patre nascitur sine matre, sic ex matre nascitur sine homine patre. Talis enim decet partus Deum." "Valde," inquit Gigas, "erubesco, quomodo virgo sine homine genuit." "Ille," inquit Rolandus, "qui fabæ gurguglionem et arboris et glisci facit gignere vermem, et multos pisces et vultures, et apes et serpentes, sine masculo semine facit parere prolem, ipse virginem intactam absque virili semine facit gignere Deum et hominem. Qui primum hominem sine alterius semine, vt dixi, fecit, facile potuit facere, vt Filius[1] homo factus de virgine sine masculo concubitu nasceretur." "Bene," inquit Ferracutus, "potest esse, quod de virgine natus fuerit : sed si Filius Dei fuit, nullatenus, vt asseris, in cruce mori potuit. Nasci, vt dicis, potuit, sed si Deus fuit, nequaquam mori potuit ; Deus enim nunquam moritur." "Bene," inquit Rolandus, "dixisti, qui de virgine nasci potuit, ecce verus homo natus fuit. Sed quia natus est vt homo, igitur mortuus est vt homo, quia qui nascitur, moritur. Si credis natiuitati, igitur crede passioni, simul et resurrectioni." "Quomodo," inquit Ferracutus, "credendum est resurrectioni ?" "Quia," inquit Rolandus, "qui nascitur, moritur ; et qui moritur, tertia die viuificatur." Tunc Gigas, audito verbo, miratus est multum, dixitque ei, "Rolande cur tot verba inania

---

[1] Ed. Filium

profers? Impossibile est, vt homo mortuus, denuo ad vitam resurgat." "Non solum," inquit Rolandus, "Dei filius à mortuis resurrexit, verum etiam omnes homines qui fuere ab initio vsque ad finem, sunt resurrecturi ante eius tribunal et accepturi meritorum suorum stipendia, prout gessit vnusquisque siue bonum, siue

malum. Ipse Deus qui modicam arborem in sublime crescere fecit, et granum frumenti mortuum in terra putrefactum reuiuiscere, crescere ac fructificare facit, ille cunctos propria carne et spiritu de morte ad vitam resuscitare in die nouissimo faciet. Leonis mysticam

tibi adsume. Si die tertio leo catulos suos mortuos hanhelitu suo viuificat, quid miraris si Deus Pater, Filium suum die tertia à mortuis resuscitauit? nec nouum tibi debet videri, si Dei Filius ad vitam rediit, cùm multi mortui ante eius resurrectionem ad vitam

rediissent. Si Helias et Elisæus facilè defunctos resuscitaverunt, facilius Deus Pater Filium resuscitauit : et ipse qui mortuos plures aute resurrectionem suam suscitavit facilè à mortuis resurrexit, et à morte nullatenus teneri potuit, ante cuius conspectum mors ipsa fugit, ad cuius vocem mortuorum phalanx resurrexit." Tunc Ferracutus, "satis," inquit, "cerno quæ dicis, sed qualiter

cœlos penetrauit, vt dixisti, prorsus ignoro." "Ille," inquit Rolandus, "qui de cœlis descendit, polos facilè ascendit : qui facilè per semetipsum resurrexit, facile polos penetrauit. Exempla multarum rerum tibi assume : vide rotam molendini quantum ad ima de supernis descendit, tantum de infimis ad sublimia ascendit. Auis volans in aëre quantum ascendit, tan-

tum descendit. Tu ipse, si forte de quodam descendisti monte, bene potes iterum redire vnde descendisti. Sol ab Oriente heri surrexit, et ad Occidentem occubuit, hodie in eodem loco surrexit. Vnde ergo filius Dei

venit, illuc rediit." "Tali igitur pacto," inquit Ferracutus, "tecum pugnabo ; quod si vera est hæc fides quam asseris, ego victus sim; et si mendax est, tu victus sis; et sit genti victæ iugiter opprobrium, victoribus autem laus et decus in æuum." "Fiat," inquit Rolandus, "ita." Bellum ex vtroque corroboratur, et illico Rolandus paganum aggreditur. Tunc Ferracutus eiecit ictum spatha sua super Rolandum, sed ipse Rolandus saltavit ad læuam, et accepit ictum spathæ in baculo suo. Interea abscisso baculo Rolandi, irruit in eum ipse Gigas, et illum arripiens leuiter inclinauit subter se ad terram. Statim agnouit Rolandus, quod tunc nullo modo euadere poterat, cœpit igitur implorare auxilium filium beatæ Mariæ semper virginis, et erexit se Deo iuuante paulatim, et reuoluit eum subter se, et adiunxit manum suam ad mucronem eius, et punxit eius parumper per vmbilicum, et euasit ab eo. Tunc excelsa voce cœpit Deum suum Gigas inuocare, dicens : "Mahumet, Mahumet, Deus meus, succurre mihi, quia morior ! Et statim ad hanc vocem concurrentes Saraceni rapuerunt eum, portantes manibus suis versus oppidum. Rolandus vero iam incolumis ad suos redierat. Illico Christiani Saracenos qui Ferracutum deferebant in oppidum, quod erat super vrbem ingenti impetu ingrediuntur. Sicque Gigas perimitur, vrbs et castra capiuntur,[1] et pugnatores à carcere eripiuntur.

glory of our faiths."

Roland attacks Ferragus, who, with a stroke of his sword, cuts Roland's staff in two, and then throws him on the ground and falls on him.

Roland prays for help to God, and, contriving to turn himself, stabs Ferragus in the navel and escapes.

The Saracen calls on his gods for help, and his countrymen come out to rescue him, but they are attacked by the Christians and defeated, and the city taken.

[1] Ed. urbem et castrum capitur.

Rauf Coilʒear.

The Taill of
RAUF COIL3EAR.

In the cheiftyme of Charlis, that chosin Chiftane,   *In the reign of Charles [the Great],*
   Thair fell ane ferlyfull flan within thay fellis wide,
Quhair Empreouris and Erlis and vther mony ane
   Turnit fra Sanct Thomas befoir the 3ule tyde.
Thay past vnto Paris, thay proudest in pane,   5
   With mony Prelatis & Princis, that was of mekle   *he and his retinue*
     pryde ;
All thay went with the king to his worthy wane,
   Ouir the feildis sa fair thay fure be his syde.   *rode out into the country.*
All the worthiest went in the morning ;
       Baith Dukis and Duchepeiris,   10
       Barrounis and Bacheleiris,
       Mony stout man steiris
       Of town with the King.

And as that Ryall raid ouir the rude mure,   *On the wild moor*
   Him betyde ane tempest that tyme, hard I tell,   15
The wind blew out of the Eist stiflie and sture,
   The deip durandlie draif in mony deip dell ;   *they were over-taken*
Sa feirslie fra the Firmament, sa fellounlie it fure,
   Thair micht na folk hald na fute on the heich fell
In point thay war to parische, thay proudest men and   *by a fearful tempest,*
     pure,   20
In thay wickit wedderis thair wist nane to dwell.
Amang thay myrk Montanis sa madlie thay mer,   *which dispersed them*
       Be it was pryme of the day,
       Sa wonder hard fure thay
       That ilk ane tuik ane seir way,   25   *in all directions.*
       And sperpellit full fer.

Ithand wedderis of the eist draif on sa fast,
 It all to-blaisterit and blew that thairin baid.
Be thay disseuerit sindrie, midmorne was past;

 Thair wist na Knicht of *the* Court quhat way *the*
  King raid.   30
He saw thair was na better bot God at the last,
 His steid aganis the storme staluartlie straid;
He Cachit fra the Court, sic was his awin cast,

 Quhair na body was him about, be fiue mylis braid.
In thay Montanis, I-wis, he wox all will,   35
  In wickit wedderis and wicht,
  Amang thay Montanis on hicht:

  Be that it drew to the nicht
  The Kyng lykit ill.

Euill lykand was the Kyng it nichtit him sa lait, 40
  And he na harberie had for his behufe;

Sa come thair ane cant Carll chachand the gait,
 With ane Capill and twa Creillis cuplit abufe.
The King carpit to the Carll withouten debait,   44

 " Schir, tell me thy richt name, for the Rude lufe :"
He sayis, " men callis me Rauf Coil3ear, as I weill wait ;
 I leid my life in this land mith mekle vnrufe,
Baith tyde and tyme, in all my trauale ;

  Hine ouir seuin mylis I dwell,
  And leidis Coilis to sell,   50
  Sen thow speris, I the tell
  All the suith hale."

" Sa mote I thrife," said the King, " I speir for nane ill ;
 Thow semis ane nobill fallow, thy answer is sa fyne."

" Forsouth," said the Coil3ear, " traist quhen thow will,
 For I trow and it be nocht swa, sum part salbe thyne."

" Mary, God forbid !" said the King, " that war bot
  lytill skill ;
Baith myself and my hors is reddy for to tyne :

I pray the, bring me to sum rest, the weddir is sa schill,
   For I defend that we fall in ony fechtine.   60
I had mekill mair nait, sum freindschip to find ;
      And gif thow can better than I,
      For the name of Sanct Iuly,
      Thow bring me to sum harbery,
        And leif me not behind !"   65

"I wait na worthie harberie heir neir-hand
   For to serue sic ane man as me think the :
Nane bot mine awin house, maist in this land,
   Fer furth in the Forest, amang the fellis hie.
With thy thow wald be payit of sic as thow fand,   70
   Forsuith thow suld be wel-cum to pas hame with me,
Or ony vther gude fallow that I heir fand
   Walkand will of his way, as me think the ;
For the wedderis ar sa fell, that fallis on the feild."
      The King was blyth quhair he raid,   75
      Of the grant that he had maid,
      Sayand, with hert glaid,
        " Schir, God 3ow for3eild ! "

" Na ! thank me not ouir airlie, for dreid that we threip,
   For I haue seruit the 3it of lytill thing to rufe ;   80
For nouther hes thow had of me fyre, drink, nor meit,
   Nor nane vther eismentis for trauellouris behufe.
Bot, micht we bring this harberie this nicht weill to
     heip,
   That we micht with ressoun baith thus excuse,
To-morne, on the morning, quhen thow sall on leip,   85
   Pryse at the parting, how that thow dois ;
For first to lofe, and syne to lak, Peter ! it is schame."
      The King said, " in gud fay,
      Schir, it is suith that 3e say."
      Into sic talk fell thay,   90
        Quhill thay war neir hame.

To the Coilƺearis hous baith, or thay wald blin,
   The Carll had Cunning weill quhair tho gait lay :

"Vndo the dure beliue ! Dame, art thow in ?
   Quhy Deuill makis thow na dule for this euill day ?
For my Gaist and I baith cheueris with the chin,   96
   Sa fell ane wedder feld I neuer, be my gude fay !"
The gude wyfe [was] glaid with the gle to begin—
   For durst scho neuer sit summoundis that scho hard
      him say—

The Carll was wantoun of word, and wox wonder wraith.
     All abaisit for blame,   101
     To the Dure went our Dame,

     Scho said, " Schir ƺe ar welcome hame,
     And ƺour Gaist baith."

" Dame, I haue deir coft all this dayis hyre,   105
   In wickit wedderis and weit walkand full will ;

Dame, kyith I am cummin hame, and kendill on ane
    fyre ;
I trow our Gaist be the gait hes farne als ill.
Ane Ryall rufe het fyre war my desyre,
   To fair the better, for his saik, gif we micht win
    thair-till ;   110

Knap doun Capounis of the best, but in the byre,
   Heir is bot hamelie fair, do beliue, Gill."
Twa cant knaifis of his awin haistelie he bad :
     " The ane of ƺow my Capill ta,
     The vther his Coursour alswa ;   115

     To the stabill swyith ƺe ga."
     Than was the King glaid.

The Coilƺear gudlie in feir, tuke him be the hand,
   And put him befoir him, as ressoun had bene ;

Quhen thay come to the dure, the King begouth to
    stand,   120
   To put the Coilƺear in befoir, maid him to mene.

He said, "thow art vncourtes, that sall I warrand!"
  He tyt the King be the nek, twa part in tene,
"Gif thow at bidding suld be boun or obeysand,
    And gif thow of Courtasie couth, thow hes for3et it
      clene! 125
Now is anis," said the Coil3ear, "kynd aucht to creip,
      Sen ellis thow art vnknawin,
      To mak me Lord of my awin;
      Sa mot I thriue, I am thrawin,
        Begin we to threip." 130

Than benwart thay 3eid, quhair brandis was bricht,
  To ane bricht byrnand fyre, as the Carll bad.
He callit on Gyliane his wyfe, thair Supper to dicht;
  "Of the best that thair is, help that we had,
[. 135
  . . . . *no break in the old edition.*]
Eftir ane euill day to haue ane mirrie nicht,
  For sa troublit with stormis was I neuer stad.
Of ilk airt of the Eist sa laithly it laid,
      3it I was mekle willar than, 140
      Quhe*n* I met with this man."
      Of sic taillis thay began,
        Quhill *the* supper was graid.

Sone was the Supper dicht, and the fyre bet,
  And thay had weschin, I-wis, the worthiest was thair:
"Tak my wyfe be the hand in feir, withowtin let, 146
  And gang begin the buird," said the Coil3ear.
"That war vnsemand, forsuith, and thy self vnset:"
The King profferit him to gang, and maid ane strange
    fair,
"Now is twyse," said the Carll, "me think thow hes
    for3et!" 150
  He leit gyrd to the King, withoutin ony mair,
And hit him vnder the eir with his richt hand,

[A iiij]

Quhill he stakkerit thair with all
   Half the breid of the hall ;
He faind neuer of ane fall,   155
   Quhill he the eird fand.

He start vp stoutly agane—vneis micht he stand—
   For anger of that outray that he had thair tane.
He callit on Gyliane his wyfe, " ga, tak him by the hand,
   And gang agane to the buird, quhair ꝫe suld air haue
      gane."   160

" Schir, thow art vnskilfull, and that sall I warrand ;
   Thow byrd to haue nurtour aneuch, and thow hes
      nane ;
Thow hes walkit, I wis, in mony wyld land,
   The mair vertew thow suld haue, to keip the fra blame !
Thow suld be courtes of kynd, and ane cunnand
   Courteir.   165

   Thocht that I simpill be,
   Do as I bid the,

   The hous is myne, pardie,
     And all that is heir."

The king said to him self, " this is ane euill lyfe,   170
   Ꝫit was I neuer in my lyfe thus-gait leird ;
And I haue oft tymes bene quhair gude hes bene ryfe,
   That maist couth of courtasie, in this Christin eird.
Is nane so gude as leif of, and mak na mair stryfe,

   For I am stonischit at this straik, that hes me thus
     steird."   175

In feir fairlie he foundis, with the gude wyfe,
   Quhair the Coilꝫear bad, sa braithlie he beird.

Quhen he had done his bidding, as him gude thocht,
   Down he sat the King neir,
   And maid him glaid & gude cheir,   180

   And said, " ꝫe ar welcum heir,
     Be him *that* me bocht."

Quhen thay war seruit and set to the Suppar,   At supper
    Gyll and the gentill King, Charlis of micht,
Syne on the tother syde sat the Coil3ear,   185
    Thus war thay marschellit but mair, & matchit that
      nicht.
Thay brocht breid to the buird, and braun of ane bair,   there was good
    And the worthyest wyne, went vpon hicht ;   cheer :
Thay Beirnis, as I wene, thay had aneuch thair,
    Within that burelie bigging, byrnand full bricht. 190
Syne enteris thair daynteis, on deis dicht dayntelie ;
      Within that worthy wane
      Forsuith wantit thay nane.   they wanted for
      With blyith cheir sayis Gyliane,   nothing.
        " Schir, dois glaidlie."   195

The Carll carpit to the King cumlie and cleir :   Rauf says the
    " Schir, the Forestaris, forsuith, of this Forest,   King's foresters
                                         threaten him on
Thay haue me all at Inuy, for dreid of the Deir ;   account of the
                                         royal Deer which
    Thay threip that I thring doun of the fattest.   he kills,
Thay say, I sall to Paris, thair to compeir   200
    Befoir our cumlie King, in dule to be drest ;
Sir manassing thay me mak, forsuith, ilk 3eir,   but he will have
                                         as many as he
    And 3it aneuch sall I haue for me and ane Gest.   wants in spite of
                                         them.
Thairfoir sic as thow seis, spend on, and not spair."
      Thus said gentill Charlis the Mane   205   Charlemagne
      To the Coil3ear agane :   remarks that the
                                         King himself has
      " The King him self hes bene fane,   on a time been
                                         glad of such
        Sum tyme, of sic fair."   cheer.

Of Capounis and Cunningis they had plentie,
    With wyne at thair will, and eik Vennysoun ;   210   [B j]
Byrdis bakin in breid, the best that may be ;
    Thus full freschlie thay fure into fusoun.
The Carll with ane cleir voce carpit on he,
    Said, " Gyll, lat the cop raik for my bennysoun,   Rauf bids his wife
                                               send the Cup
And gar our Gaist begin, and syne drink thow to me ;   round.

Sen he is ane stranger, me think it ressoun."   216

They drank dreichlie about, thay wosche and thay rais ;
     The King with ane blyith cheir
     Thankit the Coilʒeir ;
     Syne all the thre into feir   220
     To the fyre gais.

Quhen they had maid thame eis, the Coilʒear tald
   Mony sindrie taillis efter Suppair.
Ane bricht byrnand fyre was byrnand full bald ;
   The King held gude countenance, and company bair,
And euer to his asking ane answer he ʒald ;   226
   Quhill at the last he began to frane farther mair,
"In faith, freind, I wald wit, tell gif ʒe wald,
   Quhair is thy maist wynning ?" said the Coilʒear.
"Out of weir," said the King, "I wayndit neuer to tell ;
     With my Lady the Quene   231
     In office maist haue I bene,
     All thir ʒeiris fyftene,
     In the Court for to dwell."

" Quhat-kin office art thow in, quhen thow art at hame,
   Gif thow dwellis with the Quene, proudest in pane ?"
"Ane Chyld of hir Chalmer, Schir, be Sanct Jame,
   And thocht my self it say, maist inwart of ane ;
For my dwelling to nicht, I dreid me for blame."
   "Quhat sall I call *the*," said *the* Coilʒear, "quhen
     thow art hyne gane ?"   240
"Wymond of the Wardrop is my richt Name ;
   Quhair euer thow findis me befoir the, *thi* harberie is
     tane.
And thow will cum to the Court, this I vnderta,
     Thow sall haue for thy Fewaill,
     For my sake, the better saill,   245
     And onwart to thy trauaill,
     Worth ane laid or twa."

Supper ended,

they return to the fireside.

Rauf tells many tales,

and at last asks his guest where he lives.

"With the Queen," is the answer.

"What is your office with her ?"

"A gentleman of her bed-chamber.

My name is Wymond of the Wardrobe.

If you will come to court [B j, back]

I will find you good sale for your fuel."

IIe said, " I haue na knawledge quhair the Court lyis, Rauf does not know where the Court is,
  And I am wonder wa to cum quhair I am vnkend."
" And I sall say thee the suith on ilk syde, I wis, 250
  That thow sall wit weill aneuch or I fra the wend :
Baith the King and the Quene meitis in Paris but is told, and pressed to come.
  For to hald thair 3ule togidder, for scho is efter send.
Thair may thow sell, be ressoun, als deir as thow will
     prys ;
  And 3it I sall help the, gif I ocht may amend, 255
For I am knawin with Officiaris in cais thow cum thair.
     Haue gude thocht on my Name,
     And speir gif I be at hame,
     For I suppois, be Sanct Jame,
      Thow sall the better fair." 260

" Me think it ressoun, be the Rude, that I do thy red, He agrees:
  In cais I cum to the Court, and knaw bot the ane ;
Is nane sa gude as drink, and gang to our bed, and they drink and retire.
  For als far as I wait, the nicht is furth gane."
To ane preuie Chalmer beliue thay him led, 265
  Quhair ane burely bed was wrocht in that wane ;
Closit with Courtingis, and cumlie cled,
  Of the worthiest wyne wantit thay nane.
The Coil3ear and his wyfe baith with him thay 3eid, The Collier and his wife see him to bed.
     To serue him all at thay mocht, 270
     Till he was in bed brocht.
     Mair the King spak nocht,
      Bot thankit *th*ame *th*air deid.

Vpoun the morne airlie, quhen it was day, Early in the morning,
  The King buskit him sone, with scant of Squyary. the King dresses,
Wachis and Wardroparis all war away, 276 without help of attendants.
  That war wont for to walkin mony worthy.
Ane Pauyot preuilie brocht him his Palfray, [B ij]
He mounts his
  The King thocht lang of this lyfe, and lap on in hy ; palfray,
Than callit he on the Carll, anent quhair he lay, 280 and awakens Rauf

to take his leave.

For to tak his leif, than spak he freindly.
Than walkinnit thay baith, and hard he was thair :
 The Carll start vp sone,
 And prayit him to abyde none :
 " Quhill thir wickit wedderis be done   285
 I red nocht 3e fair."

The Churl would
fain detain him,

" Sa mot I thriue," said the King, "me war laith to byde ;
 Is not the morne 3ule day, formest of the 3eir ?
Ane man that Office suld beir be tyme at this tyde,
 He will be found in his fault, that wantis foroutin
  weir.   290
I se the Firmament fair vpon ather syde,
 I will returne to the Court, quhill the wedder is cleir ;
Call furth the gude wyfe, lat pay hir or we ryde,
 For the worthie harberie that I haue fundin heir."
" Lat be, God forbid," the Coil3ear said,   295
 " And thow of Charlis cumpany,
 Cheif King of Cheualry,
 That for ane nichtis harbery
 Pay suld be laid."

but the King says
he must go to his
duties.

He wants to pay
the good-wife,

but the Collier
scouts the idea.

" 3ea, sen it is sa that thow will haue na pay,   300
 Cum the morne to the Court, and do my counsall :
Deliuer the, and bring ane laid, and mak na delay,
 Thow may not schame with thy Craft, gif thow
  thriue sall.
Gif I may helf the ocht to sell, forsuith I sall assay,
 And als my self wald haue sum of the Fewall." 305
" Peter !" he said, " I sall preif the morne, gif I may,
 To bring Coillis to the Court, to se quhen thay sell sall."
" Se that thow let nocht, I pray the," said the King.
 " In faith," said the Coil3ear,
 " Traist weill I salbe thair,   310
 For thow will neuer gif the mair
 So mak ane lesing."

The guest presses
him then to
bring a load of
fuel to the Court.

The Collier will
do so to see how
coals sell.

" Bot tell me now lelely quhat is thy richt name ?
　I will forʒet the morne, and ony man me greif."
" Wymond of the Wardrop, I bid not to lane ;　315
　Tak gude tent to my name, the Court gif thow will
　　preif."
" That I haue said, I sall hald, and that I tell the plane ;
　Quhair ony Coilʒear may enchaip I trow till encheif."
Quhen he had grantit him to cum, than was the King
　fane,　319
　And withoutin ony mair let, than he tuke his leif.
Then the Coilʒear had greit thocht on the cunnand he
　had maid ;
　　　　Went to the Charcoill in hy,
　　　　To mak his Chauffray reddy ;
　　　　Agane the morne airly
　　　　　He ordanit him ane laid.　325

The lyft lemit vp beliue, and licht was the day ;
　The King had greit knawledge the countrie to ken.
Schir Rolland and Oliuer come rydand the way,
　With thame ane thousand, and ma, of fensabill men
War wanderand all the nicht ouir, & mony ma than thay
　On ilk airt outwart war ordanit sic ten,　331
Gif thay micht heir of the King, or happin quhair he lay ;
　To Jesus Christ thay pray that grace thame to len.
Als sone as Schir Rolland saw it was the King,
　　　　He kneillit doun in the place,　335
　　　　Thankand God ane greit space,
　　　　Thair was ane meting of grace
　　　　　At that gaddering.

The gentill Knicht, Schir Rolland, he kneillit on his kne,
　Thankand greit God that mekill was of micht ;　340
Schir Oliuer at his hand, and Bischoppis thre,
　Withoutin commounis that come, and mony vther
　　Knicht.

Than to Paris thay pas, all that Cheualrie,
  Betuix none of the day and 3ule nicht ;

The gentill Bischop Turpine cummand thay se,   345
  With threttie Conuent of Preistis reuest at ane sicht,
Preichand of Prophecie in Processioun.
      Efter thame baith fer and neir
      Folkis following in feir,
      Thankand God with gude cheir   350
      Thair Lord was gane to toun.

Quhen thay Princis appeirit into Paris,
  Ilk Rew Ryallie with riches thame arrayis.

Thair was Digne seruice done at Sanct Dyonys,
  With mony proud Prelat, as the buik sayis.   355
Syne to Supper thay went, within the Palys ;
  Befoir that mirthfull man menstrallis playis ;
Mony wicht wyfis sone, worthie and wise,
  Was sene at that semblay ane and twentie dayis,
With all-kin principall plentie for his plesance.   360

      Thay callit it the best 3ule than,
      And maist worthie began,
      Sen euer King Charlis was man,
      Or euer was in France.

Than vpon the morne airlie, quhen the day dew,   365
  The Coil3ear had greit thocht quhat he had vnder tane ;

He kest twa Creillis on ane Capill, with Coillis anew,
  Wandit thame with widdeis, to wend on that wane.
" Mary, it is not my counsall, but 3one man that 3e knew,
  To do 3ow in his gentrise," said Gyliane ;   370

"Thow gaif him ane outragious blaw, & greit boist blew;
  In faith thow suld haue bocht it deir, & he had bene
    allane.
For thy, hald 3ow fra the Court, for ocht that may be ;
      3one man that thow outrayd
      Is not sa simpill as he said ;   375

      Thairun my lyfe dar I layd,
      That sall thow heir and se."

“ 3ea, Dame, haue nane dreid of my lyfe to day ;

    Lat me wirk as I will, the weird is mine awin.

I spak not out of ressoun, the suth gif I sall say,   380

    To Wymond of the Wardrop, war the suith knawin.

That I haue hecht I sall hald, happin as it may,

    Quhidder sa it gang to greif or to gawin.”

He caucht twa Creillis on ane capill, & catchit on his way

    Ouir the Daillis sa derf, be the day was dawin.   385

The hie way to Paris, in all that he mocht,

        With ane quhip in his hand,

        Cantlie on catchand ;

        To fulfill his cunnand,

           To the Court socht.   390

Graith thocht of the grant had the gude King,

    And callit Schir Rolland him till, and gaif command-

      ment,

(Ane man he traistit in, maist atour all vther thing,

    That neuer wald set him on assay withoutin his assent,)

“ Tak thy hors and thy harnes in the morning ;   395

    For to watche weill the wayis, I wald that thow went,

Gif thow meitis ony leid lent on the ling,

    Gar thame boun to this Burgh, I tell the mine Intent.

Or gyf thow seis ony man cumming furth the way,

        Quhat sumeuer that he be,   400

        Bring him haistely to me,

        Befoir none that I him se

        In this hall the day.”

Schir Rolland had greit ferly, and in hart kest

    Quhat that suld betakin, that the King tald.   405

Vpon solempnit 3ule day, quhen ilk man suld rest,

    That him behouit neidlingis to watche on the wald,

Quhen his God to serue he suld haue him drest.

    And syne, with ane blyith cheir, buskit that bald,

Out of Paris proudly he preikit full prest ;   410

    In till his harnes all haill his hechtis for to hald,

He vmbekest the countrie, outwith the toun.
  He saw na thing on steir,
  Nouther fer nor neir,
  Bot the feildis in feir,   415
  Daillis and doun.

He huit and he houerit quhill midmorne and mair,
  Behaldand the hie hillis and passage sa plane;

Sa saw he quhair the Coil3ear come with all his fair,
  With twa Creillis on ane Capill; thairof was he
   fane.   420
He followit to him haistely, amang the holtis hair,
  For to bring him to the king, at bidding full bane.

Courtesly to the Knicht kneillit the Coil3ear,
  And Schir Rolland him self salust him agane,
Syne bad him leif his courtasie, and boun him to ga; 425

  He said, "withoutin letting,
  Thow mon to Paris to the King;
  Speid the fast in ane ling,
  Sen I find na ma."

"In faith," said the Coil3ear, "3it was I neuer sa
  nyse;   430
Schir Knicht, it is na courtasie commounis to scorne:
Thair is mony better than I, cummis oft to Parys,
  That the King wait not of, nouther nicht nor morne.

For to towsill me or tit me, thocht foull be my clais,
  Or I be dantit on sic wyse, my lyfe salbe lorne." 435

"Do way," said Schir Rolland, "me think thow art not
  wise,
I red thow at bidding be, be all that we haue sworne;
And call thow it na scorning, bot do as I the ken,
  Sen thow has hard mine Intent:
  It is the Kingis commandement,   440

  At this tyme thow suld haue went
  And I had met sic ten."

"I am bot ane mad man, that thow hes heir met;
   I haue na myster to matche with maisterfull men.
Fairand ouir the feildis, Fewell to fet,   445   The Collier
   And oft fylit my feit in mony foull fen;   will go
Gangand with laidis, my gouerning to get.
   Thair is mony Carll in the countrie thow may nocht
      ken;
I sall hald that I haue hecht, bot I be hard set,
   To Wymond of the Wardrop, I wait full weill   [B iiij, back]
      quhen."   450 the Wardrobe;
"Sa thriue I," said Rolland, "it is mine Intent   but Roland says
      That nouther to Wymond nor Will   he shall go to the
      Thow sald hald nor hecht till,   King first.
      Quhill I haue brocht the to fulfill
      The Kingis commandment."   455

The Carll beheld to the Knicht, as he stude than;   The Churl looks
   He bair grauit in Gold, and Gowlis in grene,   at the Knight's
Glitterand full gaylie quhen Glemis began,   array:
   Ane Tyger ticht to ane tre, ane takin of tene.
Trewlie that tenefull was trimland than,   460
   Semelie schapin and schroud in that Scheild schene;
Mekle worschip of weir worthylie he wan,
   Befoir, into fechting with mony worthie sene.
His Basnet was bordourit, and burneist bricht   his basnet
      With stanes of Beriall cleir,   465 gleaming
      Dyamountis and Sapheir,   with precious
      Riche Rubeis in feir,   stones,
      Reulit full richt.

His plaitis properlie picht attour with precious stanis,
   And his Pulanis full prest of that ilk peir;   470
Greit Graipis of Gold his Greis for the nanis,
   And his Cussanis cumlie schynand full cleir.
Bricht braissaris of steill about his arme banis,   his armour
   Blandit with Beriallis and Cristallis cleir,

Ticht ouir with Thopas, and trew lufe atanis ;　　475
　　The teind of his Iewellis to tell war full teir.

His Sadill circulit and set, richt sa on ilk syde ;
　　　　His brydill bellisand and gay,
　　　　His steid stout on stray,
　　　　He was the Ryallest of array,　　480
　　　　　On Ronsy micht ryde.

Of that Ryall array that Rolland in raid
　　Rauf rusit in his hart of that Ryall thing ;
" He is the gayest in geir, that euer on ground glaid ;
　　Haue he grace to the gre in ilk Iornaying.　　485
War he ane manly man, as he is weill maid,
　　He war full michtie, with magre durst abyde his
　　　meting."
He bad the Coilȝear in wraith swyth withoutin baid,
　　Cast the Creillis fra the Capill, and gang to the King.
" In faith, it war greit schame," said the Coilȝear ; 490
　　　　" I vndertuk thay suld be brocht,
　　　　This day for ocht that be mocht ;
　　　　Schir Knicht that word is for nocht
　　　　　That thow Carpis thair ! "

" Thow huifis on thir holtis, and haldis me heir,　　495
　　Quhill half the haill day may the hicht haue."
" Be Christ that was Cristinnit, and his Mother cleir,
　　Thow sall catche to the Court that sall not be to craue.
It micht be preisit preiudice, bot gif thow suld compeir,
　　To se quhat granting of grace the King wald the gaif."
" For na gold on this ground wald I, but weir,　　501
　　Be fundin fals to the King, sa Christ me saue ! "
" To gar the cum and be knawin, as I am command,
　　　　I wait not quhat his willis be,
　　　　Nor he namit na mair the,　　505
　　　　Nor ane vther man to me,
　　　　　Bot quhome that I fand."

" Thow fand me fechand nathing that followit to feid,   *The Collier undaunted*
  I war ane fule gif I fled, and fand nane affray :
Bot as ane lauch-full man, my laidis to leid,   510
  That leifis with mekle lawtie and laubour in fay.
Be the Mother and the Maydin that maid vs remeid,
  And thow mat me ony mair, cum efter quhat sa may,
Thow I sall dyntis deill, quhill ane of vs be deid,   *threatens him with dints for his interference,*
  For the deidis thow hes me done vpon this deir day."
Mekle merwell of that word had Schir Rolland ;   516
      He saw na wappinnis thair,   *at which Sir Roland, seeing no weapons,*
      That the Coil3ear bair,
      Bot ane auld Buklair,
        And ane roustie brand.   520

" It is lyke," said Schir Rolland, and lichtly he leuch,   *[Cj, back] laughs lightly.*
  " That sic ane stubill husband man wald stryke
    stoutly ;
Thair is mony toun man, to tuggill is full teuch,
  Thocht thair brandis be blak and vnburely ;
Oft fair foullis ar fundin faynt, and als freuch.   525 *He objects to fighting,*
  I defend we fecht or fall in that foly ;
Lat se how we may disseuer with sobernes aneuch,
  And catche crabitnes away, be Christ counsall I.
Quhair winnis that Wymond thow hecht to meit *and learning that Wymond dwells*
  to day ? "
      " With the Quene, tauld he me ;   530 *with the Queen,*
      And thair I vndertuke to be,
      Into Paris Pardie,   *in Paris,*
        Withoutin delay."

" And I am knawin with the Quene," said Schir *he says he is himself acquainted with the Queen, and her ladies.*
  Rolland,
  " And with mony byrdis in hir Bowre, be buikis and
    bellis ;   535
The King is into Paris, that sall I warrand,
  And all his aduertance that in his Court dwellis.

Me tharth haue nane noy of myne erand,
 For me think thow will be thair efter as thow tellis;
Bot gif I fand the, forrow now to keip my cunnand."
 "Schir Knicht," said *the* Coil3ear, "thow trowis me
  neuer ellis,   541
Bot gif sum suddand let put it out of delay;
  For that I hecht of my will,

  And na man threit me thair till,
  That I am haldin to fulfill,   545
  And sall do quhill I may."

"3ea, sen thow will be thair, thy cunnandis to new,
 I neid nane airar myne erand nor none of the day."
"Be thow traist," said the Coil3ear, "man, as I am trew,
 I will not haist me ane fute faster on the way; 550

Bot gif thow raik out of my renk, full raith sall
 thow rew,
 Or be the Rude I sall rais thy Ryall array;
Thocht thy body be braissit in that bricht hew,
 Thow salbe fundin als febil of thy bone fay."

Schir Rolland said to him self, "this is bot foly 555
  To striue with him ocht mair:
  I se weill he will be thair."

  His leif at the Coil3ear
  He tuke lufesumly.

"Be Christ!" said the Coil3ear, "that war ane foull
  scorne,   560
 That thow suld chaip, bot I the knew, that is sa
  schynand;
For thow seis my weidis ar auld, and all to-worne,
 Thow trowis nathing thir taillis that I am telland.

Bring na Beirnis vs by, bot as we war borne,
 And thir Blonkis that vs beiris, thairto I mak ane
  bland,   565
That I sall meit the heir vpon this mure to morne,
 Gif I be haldin in heill—and thairto my hand—

Sen that we haue na laiser at this tyme to ta."

In ane thourtour way,
Seir gaitis pas thay, 570
Baith to Paris in fay ;
Thus partit thay twa.

when he will have
leisure to tackle
him.

The gentill Knicht, Schir Rolland come rydand full
 sone,
 And left the Coil3ear to cum, as he had vndertane ;
And quhen he come to Paris the hie Mes was done,
 The King with mony cumly out of the Kirk is
 gane.
Of his harnes in hy he hynt withoutin hone, 577
 And in ane Rob him arrayit richest of ane ;
In that worschipfull weid he went in at none,
 As he was wont, with the wy that weildit the wane,
On fute ferly in feir, formest of all. 581

Sir Roland
returns to the
King,
leaving the
Collier to follow.

Richt weill payit was the King
Of Schir Rollandis cumming ;
To speir of his tything
 Efter him gart call. 585

The King is glad
to see the knight,

The King in counsall him callit, "cum hidder, Schir
 Knicht !
 Hes thow my bidding done, as I the command ? "
" In faith," said Schir Rolland, " I raid on full richt,
 To watch wyselie the wayis ; that I sall warrand.
Thair wald na douchtie this day for Iornay be dicht ;
 Fairand ouir the feildis full few thair I fand ; 591
Saif anerly ane man that semblit in my sicht,
 Thair was na leid on lyfe lent in this land."
" Quhat kin a fallow was that ane, Schir, I the pray ? "

and asks if he has
done his bidding :
Sir Roland
explains,
 [C ij, back]

that he has seen
no one,

" Ane man in husband weid, 595
Buskit busteously on breid ;
Leidand Coillis he 3eid
 To Paris the way."

save a poor man
conveying coals.

The King
reproaches him
for not bringing
that poor man.

“ Quhy hes thow not that husband brocht, as I the
     bad ?
I dreid me, sa he dantit the, thow durst not with him
     deill.”   600
“ In faith,” said Schir Rolland, “ gif that he sa had,
That war full hard to my hart, and I ane man in heill.”

Sir Roland
hastens out,

He saw the King was engreuit, and gat furth glaid,
     To se gif the Coilȝearis lawtie was leill :   604
“ I suld haue maid him in the stour to be full hard stad,
And I had witten that the Carll wald away steill ;
Bo[t] I trowit not the day that he wald me beget.”
          As he went outwart bayne,

and meets a
porter,

          He met ane Porter swayne
          Cummand raith him agayne,   610
            Fast fra the ȝet.

“ Quhair gangis thow, Gedling, thir gaitis sa gane ? ”

who says that a
Collier is

     “ Be God,” said the Grome, “ane gift heir I geif ;
I deuise at the ȝet thair is ane allane,
     Bot he be lattin in beliue, him lykis not to leif. 615

clamouring to be
let in at the
palace gate.

With ane Capill and twa Creillis cassin on the plane,
     To cum to this Palice he preissis to preif.”
“ Gif thow hes fundin that Freik, in faith I am fane ;
     Lat him in glaidly, it may not engreif.

Sir Roland bids
the porter

Bot askis he eirnestly efter ony man ? ”   620
          Than said the Gedling on ground :
          “ ȝe, forsuith in this stound,
          Efter ane Wymound
          In all that he can.”

[C iij]
admit him
quickly to seek
for Wymond.

“ Pas agane, Porter, and let him swyith in,   625
     Amang the proudest in preis, plesand in pane.
Say thow art not worthy to Wymond to win,
     Bid him seik him his self, gif thair be sic ane.”
Agane gangis Schir Rolland, quhair gle suld begin,
     And the ȝaip ȝeman to the ȝet is gane ;   630

Enbraissit the bandis beliue or that he wald blin,
 Syne leit the wy at his will wend in the wane.
"Gang seik him now thy self," he said vpon hicht :
   "My self hes na lasair
   Fra thir 3ettis to fair."   635
    " Be Christ," said the Coil3ear,
    "I set that bot licht."

" Gif thow will not seik him, my awin self sall :
 For I haue oft tymes swet in seruice full fair.
Tak keip to my Capill, that na man him call, 640
 Quhill I cum fra the Court," said the Coil3ear.
" My laid war I laith to lois, I leif the heir all ;
 Se that thow leis thame not, bot 3eme thame full 3air."
In that hardy in hy, he haiket to that hall,
 For to wit gif Wymondis wynning was thair. 645
He arguit with the Ischar ofter than anis,
   " Schir, can thow ocht say
   Quhair is Wymond the day ?
   I pray the, bring him gif thow may
    Out of this wanis."   650

He trowit that the wy had wittin of Wymond he wend,
 Bot to his raifand word he gaue na reward ;
Thair was na man thairin that his name kend,
 Thay countit not the Coil3ear almaist at regaird.
He saw thair was na meiknes nor mesure micht mend,
 He sped him in spedely, and nane of thame he spaird ;
Thair was na fyue of thay Freikis, that micht him furth
  send,
 He socht in sa sadly, quhill sum of thame he saird.
He thristit in throw thame thraly with threttis.
   Quhen he come amang thame all, 660
   3it was the King in the hall,
   And mony gude man with all,
    Vngane to the meit.

to where the King
is dining in state
Thocht he had socht sic ane sicht all this seuin 3eir,
  Sà solempnit ane semblie had he not sene ; 665
The hall was properly apperrellit and paintit but peir,
  Dyamountis full dantely dentit betwene.
It was semely set on ilk syde seir,
  Gowlis glitterand full gay, glemand in grene,
in a splendid hall Flowris with Flourdelycis formest in feir, 670
  With mony flamand ferly ma than fyftene.
The rufe reulit about in reuall of Reid,
   Rois reulit Ryally,
   Columbyn and Lely ;
   Thair was ane hailsum harbery 675
   Into riche steid.

With Dosouris to the duris dicht, quha sa wald deme,
with all dainties,   With all diuers danteis dicht dantely ;
Circulit with siluer semely to sene,
  Selcouthly in seir he was set suttelly. 680
Blyth byrdis abufe, and bestiall full bene,
  Fyne foullis in Fyrth, and Fischis with fry ;
and adornments. The flure carpit and cled, and couerit full clene,
  Cummand fra the Cornellis closand quemely.
Bricht Bancouris about browdin ouir all, 685
   Greit Squechonis on hicht,
   Anamalit and weill dicht,
   Reulit at all richt
   Endlang the hall. 689

Rauf would fain
see Wymond
" Heir is Ryaltie," said Rauf, " aneuch for the nanis,
  With all nobilnes anournit, and that is na nay ;
Had I of Wymond ane word, I wald of thir wanis,
[C iiij]
and get away.   Fra thir wyis, I-wis, to went on my way ;
Bot I mon 3it heir mair quhat worthis of him anis,
  And eirnestly efter him haue myne E ay." 695
He thristit in throw threttie all atanis,
  Quhair mony douchtie of deid war Ioynit that day.

For he was vnburely, on bak thay him hynt;   After many
    As he gat ben throw,   rebuffs
    He gat mony greit schow;   700   and shoves,
    Bot he was stalwart, I trow,
    And laith for to stynt.

He thristit in throw thame, and thraly can thring,
  Fast to the formest he foundit in feir :   704
Sone besyde him he gat ane sicht of the Nobill   he catches sight
  King,   of the King,
    and cries,
  "3one is Wymond, I wait, it worthis na weir ;   "Yon is
    Wymond!
I ken him weill, thocht he be cled in vther clething,   I know him in
  In clais of clene gold kythand 3one cleir.   708   any clothes :

. . . .

  Quhen he harbreit with me, be half as he is heir,   but he is grander
In faith he is of mair stait, than euer he me tald.   than he led me
    Allace, that I was hidder wylit!   to expect!"
    I dreid me sair I be begylit!"
    The King preuilie smylit,   The King smiles
      at his surprise.
      Quhen he saw that bald.   715

Thair was seruit in that saill Seigis semelie,
  Mony Sen3eorabill Syre on ilk syde seir;
With ane cairfull countenance the Coil3ear kest   Rauf casts his eye
  his E   on the Queen,
  To the cumly Quene courtes and cleir :
"Dame, of thy glitterand gyde haue I na gle,   720
  Be the gracious God that bocht vs sa deir ;
To ken Kingis Courtasie, the Deuill come to me,
  And sa I hope I may say, or I chaip heir.   and says if he can
Micht I chaip of this chance, that changes my   once escape,
  cheir,
    Thair suld na man be sa wyse,   725   no man shall
      entice him here
    To gar me cum to Parise,   again!
    To luke quhair the King lyis,
    In faith, this scuin 3eir!"

[C iiij, back]
But when they leave the table, the King relates his adventure,

Quhen worthie had weschin, and fra the buirdis went,
    Thay war for-wonderit I wis of thair wyse Lord ;
The King fell in carping, and tauld his Intent,   731
    To mony gracious Grome he maid his record.

and the Collier's behaviour.

How the busteous Beirne met him on the bent,
    And how the Frostis war sa fell, and sa strait ford.

Rauf quakes,

Than the CoilꝜear quoke as he had bene schent,   735
    Quhen he hard the suith say how he the King schord.

and wishes rather that he had the King alone on the moor—or the best of his Knights.

"Greit God ! gif I war now, and thy self with all,
    Vpon the mure quhair we met,
    Baith all suddandly set,
    Or ony Knicht that thow may get   740
    Sa gude in thy hall !"

The lords laugh loud;

Thir Lordis leuch vpon loft, and lystinit to the King,
    How he was ludgeit and led, and set at sa licht ;

the Knights bid hang him.

Than the curagious Knichtis bad haue him to hing,
    "For he hes seruit that," thay said, "be our sicht."

"God forbid !" quoth the King ;

"God forbot," he said, "my thank war sic thing   746
    To him that succourit my lyfe in sa euill ane nicht !
Him semis ane stalwart man, and stout in stryking,

"he shall be knighted himself!"

    That Carll for his Courtasie salbe maid knicht.
I hald the counsall full euill that Cristin man slais,
    For I had myster to haue ma,   751
    And not to distroy tha
    Tha[t] war worthie to ga
    To fecht on Goddis fais !"

He dubs him on the spot,

Befoir mony worthie he dubbit him Knicht,   755
    Dukis and digne Lordis in that deir hall.
" Schir, se for thy self, thow semis to be wicht ;
    Tak keip to this ordour, ane Knicht I the call ;
To mak the manly man, I mak the of micht,

assigns him a revenue, and promises the next vacant fief

    Ilk Ꝝeir thre hundreth pund assigne the I sall.   760
And als the nixt vacant, be ressonabill richt,
    That hapnis in France, quhair sa euer it fall,

Forfaltour or fre waird, that first cummis to hand,
    I gif the heir heritabilly,
      Sa that I heir, quhen I haue hy,   765
      That thow be fundin reddy
        With Birny & brand."

  "It war my will, worthy, thy schone that thow wan,
    And went with thir weryouris wythest in weir;
Heir ar curagious Knichtis, suppois thay the nocht
    ken,
    For thy simpill degre that thow art in heir.   771
I beseik God of his grace to mak the ane gude man,
    And I sall gif the to begin glitterand geir."
Ane Chalmer with Armour the King gart richt than
    Betaucht to ane Squyar, and maid him keipeir.
With clois Armouris of steill for that stout Knicht,
      Sextie Squyaris of fee,
      Of his retinew to be;
      That was ane fair cumpany
        Schir Rauf gat that nicht.   780

Vpon the morne airly, Schir Rauf wald not rest,
    Bot in Ryall array he reddyit him to ryde;
For to hald that I haue hecht, I hope it be the
    best,
To 3one busteous Beirne that boistit me to byde.
Amang the Gal3art Gromis I am bot ane Gest,   785
    I will the ganandest gait to that gay glyde;
Sall neuer Lord lauch on loft, quhill my lyfe may
    lest,
    That I for liddernes suld leif, and leuand besyde.
It war ane graceles gude that I war cummin to,
      Gif that the King hard on hicht   790
      That he had maid ane carll Knicht
      Amang thir weryouris wicht,
        And docht nocht to do."

Vpon ane rude Runsy he ruschit out of toun ;

    In ane Ryall array he rydis full richt ;   795

Euin to the Montane he maid him full boun,

    Quhair he had trystit to meit Schir Rolland the Knicht.

Derfly ouir Daillis, discouerand the doun,

    Gif ony douchtie that day for Iornayis was dicht.

He band his blonk to ane busk on the brent broun,

    Syne baid be the bair way to hald that he had hecht.

Quhill it was neir time of the day that he had thair bene,

      He lukit ane lytill him fra,

      He sa cummand in thra

      The maist man of all tha,   805

      That euer he had sene.

Ane Knicht on ane Cameill come cantly at hand,

    With ane curagious countenance, and cruell to se ;

He semit baldly to abyde with Birny and with brand,

    His blonk was vnburely, braid and ouir hie.   810

Schir Rauf reddyit him sone, and come rydand,

    And in the rowme of ane renk in fewtir kest he ;

He seimit fer fellonar than first quhen he him fand,

    He foundis throw his forcenes gif he micht him se.

He straik the steid with the spurris, he sprent on the bent ;

      Sa hard ane cours maid thay,   816

      That baith thair hors deid lay,

      Their speiris in splenders away

      Abufe thair heid sprent.

Thus war thay for thair forcynes left on fute baith,

    Thay sture hors at that straik strikin deid lay than ;

Thir riche restles renkis ruschit out full raith,

    Cleikit out twa swordis and togidder ran.

Kest thame with gude will to do vther skaith,

    Bair on thair basnetis thay Beirnis or thay blan. 825

Haistely hewit thay togiddir, to leif thay war laith

    To tyne the worschip of weir that thay air wan ;

Na for dout of vincussing thay went nocht away.
    Thus ather vther can assaill
    With swordis of mettaill ;   830
    Thay maid ane lang battaill
      Ane hour of the day.

A long hour they fight,

Thay hard harnest men, thay hewit on in haist ;   [D ij]
  Thay worthit heuy with heid, and angerit with all ;
Quhill thay had maid thame sa mait, thay fail3e almaist,   *till both grow faint.*
  Sa laith thay war on ather part to lat thair price fall.
The riche restles men out of the renk past,   837
  Forwrocht with thair wapnis, and euill rent with all ;
Thair was na girth on the ground, quhill ane gaif *the*
     gaist ;
  " 3arne efter 3eilding," on ilk syde thay call.   840   *As each cries, "Now, think of yielding ! "*
Schir Rauf caucht to cule him, and tak mair of the licht,
    He kest vp his Veseir,
    With ane Cheualrous cheir,
    Sa saw he cummand full neir   *Rauf espies another Knight coming.*
      Ane vther kene Knicht.   845

" Now, be the Rude ! " said Schir Rauf, " I repreif the !   *He taunts his foe with broken faith,*
  Thow hes brokin conditioun, thow hes not done richt :
Thow hecht na bakheir to bring, bot anerly we ;
  Thairto I tuik thy hand, as thow was trew Knicht."   *who was to meet him alone.*
On loud said the Sara3ine, " I heir the now lie !   850   *"Thou liest," says the Saracen ;*
  Befoir the same day I saw the neuer with sicht ;
Now sall thow think it richt sone, thow hes met   *"I never saw thee before."*
    with me,
  Gif Mahoun or Termagant may mantene my micht."
Schir Rauf was blyth of that word, & blenkit with his   *Blithe is Rauf to find his foe is a Saracen.*
    face ;
    " Thow sayis thow art ane Sara3ine ?   855
    Now thankit be Drichtine,
    That ane of vs sall neuer hine,
      Vndeid in this place."

<table>
<tr><td>Neither intends
to let the other
go alive;</td><td>Than said the Saraƺine to Schir Rauf succudrously,
   "I haue na lyking to lyfe to lat the with lufe."   860
He gaue ane braid with his brand to the Beirne by,
   Till the blude of his browis brest out abufe.
The kene Knicht in that steid stakkerit sturely,
   The lenth of ane rude braid he gart him remufe.</td></tr>
</table>

Becum Christin, Schir Knicht, and on Christ call ;
  It is my will thow conuert,
  This wickit warld is bot ane start— 895
  And haue him halely in hart
   That maker is of all."

"Schir Rolland, I rek nocht of thy Rauingis ;
  Thow dois bot reuerance to thame that rekkis it
   nocht ;
Thow slane hes oft, thy self, of my Counsingis, 900
  Soudanis and sib men, that the with schame socht.
Now faindis to haue fauour with thy fleichingis,
  Now haue I ferlie, gif I fauour the ocht ;
We sall spuilƷe Ʒow dispittously at the nixt springis,
  Mak Ʒow biggingis full bair, bodword haue I brocht.
Chace Charlis Ʒour King fer out of France ; 906
   Fra the Chane of Tartarie,
   At him this message wald I be,
   To tell him as I haue tauld the,
    Withoutin plesance." 910

"Tyte tell me thy name, it seruis of nocht ;
  Ʒe SaraƷeins ar succuderus and self willit ay,
Sall neuer of sa sour ane brand ane bricht fyre be
  brocht,
  The Feynd is sa felloun als fers as he may." 914
"Sa thriue I," said the SaraƷine, "to threip is my
  thocht,
Quha waitis the Cristin with cair, my cusingis ar thay;
My name is Magog, in will and I mocht,
  To ding thame doun dourly that euer war in my way.
For thy my warysoun is full gude at hame quhair I dwel."
   "In faith," said Schir Rolland, 920
   "That is full euill wyn land
   To haue quhill thow ar leuand,
    Sine at thine end hell.

“ Wald thow conuert the in hy, and couer the of sin,
  Thow suld haue mair profite and mekle pardoun ;

Riche Douchereis seir to be sesit in,   926
  During quhill day dawis, that neuer will gang doun ;

Wed ane worthie to wyfe, and weild hir with win,
  Ane of the riche of our Realme be that ressoun ;

The gentill Duches, Dame Iane, that claimis be hir kin
  Angeos and vther landis, with mony riche toun. 931
Thus may thow, and thow will, wirk the best wise,
   I do the out of dispair,
   In all France is nane so fair

   Als scho is, appeirand air   935
   To twa Douchereis.”

“ I rek nocht of thy riches, Schir Rolland the Knicht,”
  Said the rude Sara3ine in Ryall array,
“ Thy God nor thy Grassum set I bot licht ;

  Bot gif thy God be sa gude as I heir the say,   940
I will forsaik Mahoun, and tak me to his micht,
  Euer mair perpetuallie as he that mair may.
Heir with hart and gude will my treuth I the plicht,

  That I sall lelely leif on thy Lord ay,
And I beseik him of Grace, and askis him mercy,   945

   And Christ his Sone full schene,
   For I haue Christin men sene,
   That in mony angeris hes bene,
   Full oft on him cry.”   949

“ I thank God,” said Rolland, “ that word lykis me !
  And Christ his sweit Sone, that the that grace send.”

Thay swoir on thair swordis swyftlie all thre,
  And conseruit thame freindis to thair lyfis end,
Euer in all trauell, to leif and to die.

  Thay Knichtis caryit to the court, as Christ had thame
   kend.   955

The King for thair cumming maid game and gle,
  With mony mirthfull man thair mirthis to mend.

Digne Bischoppis that day, that douchtic gart bring,
    And gaue him Sacramentis seir,
    And callit him Schir Gawteir,   960
    And sine the Duches cleir
        He weddit with ane ring.

> Bishops administer the Sacraments, name him Sir Walter, and wed him to the Duchess.

Than Schir Rauf gat rewaird to keip his Knichtheid :
    Sic tythingis come to the King within thay nyne nicht,
That the Marschell of France was newlingis deid ; 965
    Richt thair, with the counsall of mony kene Knicht,
He thocht him richt worthie to byde in his steid,
    For to weild that worschip worthie and wicht.
His wyfe wald he nocht for3et, for dout of Goddis feid.
    He send efter that hende, to leif thame in richt, 970
Syne foundit ane fair place quhair he met the King,
    Euer mair perpetually,
    In the name of Sanct Iuly,
    That all that wantis harbery,
        Suld haue gestning.   975

> Sir Rauf's Knighthood is approved, and he made maréchal of France. He duly sends for his wife, and on the spot where he met the King, founds a hospice in name of St. July.

Finis.

Imprentit at Sanc/tandrois be Robert Lekpreuik
Anno 1572

Rouland and Vernagu.

Rouland and Vernagu.

1 . . . .

    For he it seiȝe wiþ siȝt.   *[Fol. 263, col. 1.]*
Now bigin ichil of him,   *Now will I tell of*
Of charls þat was stout & grim,   *Charles, the stout*
    & tel ȝou al þat riȝt.   4   *and grim,*

2 ¶ An hundred winter it was and þre,
Seþen god dyed opon þe tre,
    þat charls þe king   7
Hadde al fraunce in his hond,   *King of Franȝe,*
Danmark & Inglond,   *Denmark, and*
    Wiþouten ani lesing,   10   *England,*
Lorein & lombardye,
Gascoun, bayoun, & pikardye,
    Was til his bidding ;   13
& emperour he was of rome,   *and Emperor of*
& lord of al christendome,   *Rome.*
    þan was he an heiȝe lording.   16

3 In þat time was an emperour   *Constantius was*
    In costentin of gret honour,   *then Emperor of*
    Constansious he hiȝt ;   19 *Constantinople,*
God he loued & alle his,
& hated hem þat dede amis,
    Wiþ al his miȝt.   22
In speyn, þo þer was a king,   *and Ebrahim*
A stern man wiþouten lesing,   *King of Spain.*
    þat werred oȝain þe riȝt.   25
Ebrahim was his name,
Wide sprong his riche fame,
    He was a douȝti kniȝt.   28

4   ¶ Alle þat leued in godes lawe,
     He lete hem boþe hong & drawe,
               þo þat he miȝt of take ;   31

     & þe patriark of ierusalem
     Out of lond he dede him flem,
               Al for godes sake.   34

     þe patriarke was ful wiis,

     & to þemperour he went y-wis,
               His mone for to make,   37
     Hou þe king ebrahim
     Out of lond exiled him,
               Wiþ michel wer & wrake.   40

5   ¶ King costance þemperour
     Made swiþe gret dolour
               For þis tidinges,   43

     Ihū crist bisouȝt he,
     Almiȝti god in trinite,
               King of al kinges,   46
     He sende him grace him to slo,
     þat had y-wrouȝt so michel wo,
               & slawe godes ginges,   49
     & sone so he had þe bon y-bede,

     An angel liȝt doun in þat stede,
               & þis bode him bringes.   52

6   ¶ þe angel seyd to þemperour,
     "Wele þe greteþ þi saueour,
               Ihū, ful of miȝt,   55

     & bit þe sende wiþ michel anour,
     After charls þe conquerour,
               He is a douhti kniȝt.   58
     He schal þe help in batayl,
     & sle þe sarrazin wiþouten fail,
               þat doþ oȝain þe riȝt."   61

     þemperour was glad & bliþe,
     & þonked god fele siþe,
               His hert nas neuer so liȝt.   64

7   ¶ Four þe best he sent of hem,
    þat on hiȝt dauid of ierusalem,
        & samuel al so,   67
    Ion of naples was anoþer,
    Ysac hiȝt þe ferþ broþer,
        þider he gan go.   70
    He went to þe palais of rome,
    & bi-for sir charli[s] come
        & told him of her wo ;   73
    þai toke him þe letter & kist his hand,
    Swiche was þe lawe of þe land,
        & schal ben euer mo.   76

He sent four envoys with a letter

to Charles at Rome.

8   ¶ Charls wepe for þat dede,
    When he herd þe letter rede,
        & hete an heiȝeing,   79
    Al þat miȝt armes bere,
    Kniif or scheld, swerd or spere,
        Men schuld bi-for him bring.   82
    þai busked hem & made hem yare,
    To costentin for to fare,
        Wiþouten ani lesing.   85
    þemperour was glad y-wis,
    & vnderfenge wiþ miche blis,
        Sir charls þe king.   88

Charles was grieved,

and ordered all who could bear arms to assemble,

and then march to Constantinople.

9   ¶ Riche iuels wiþouten lesing,
    Sir costance þe king
        Bifor sir charls he brouȝt ;   91
    Sauage bestes for þe nones,
    Gold & siluer, & riche stones,
        Ac þer of nold he nouȝt :   94
    He bi-souȝt him of more honour,
    Of ihū our saueour,
        þat al þis warld haþ wrouȝt,   97
    þat he on suffred passioun,
    Of þe croice & of þe croun,
        þer of he him bi-souȝt.   100

[fol. 263, back, col. 1.]
Constantius pre-sented Charles with jewels,

and other honours.

10   ¶ þemp*er*our his wil dede,

     & ladde him to þe holy stede,

         þere þe relikes ware ;   103

He showed him the holy relics,

     þer com swiche a swete odour,

     þat neuer ȝete so swete sauour,

         No feld þai neuer are ;   106

the very odour of which cured three hundred sick people.

     Of þe smal þat was so swote,

     þre hundred sike hadde her bote,

         & cast were out of care.   109

There were the holy crown, the arm of St. Simeon,

     þan brouȝt þai forþ þe holy croun,

     & þe arme of seyn simoun,

         Bi-forn hem alle þare.   112

a piece of the cross,

11   ¶ & a parti of þe holy crosse,

     þat in a cristal was don in clos,

         & godes cloþeing.   115

our Lady's smock,

     Our leuedi smok þ^t hye had on,

the rod of Aaron,

     & þe ȝerd of araon,

         Forþ þai gun bring,   118

the spear of Longinus,

     & a spere long & smert,

     þat longys put to godes hert,

         He gaf charls þe king ;   121

and one of the nails.

     & a nail long & gret

     þat was y-driue þurch godes fet,

         Wiþ outen ani lesing.   124

12   ¶ When charls had reseiued þat þing,

     He bisouȝt ihū, heuen king,

         To sende him miȝt & space,   127

Charles prayed for a proof of the relics,

     For to wite þe soþe þere,

     Ȝif þe relikes verray were,

         Er he þennes pase.   130

and the place was filled with a heavenly light.

     þan decended a liȝtnesse,

     Doun riȝtes fram þe heuen blis,

         In þat ich place,   133

[fol. 263, back, col. 2.]

     þat þai wenden alle y-wis,

     þai hadde ben in paradys,

         So ful it was of grace.   136

13   ¶ þai tok leue at þemper̄our,
     & þonked him of gret honour,
         & to aise in gascoyn went ;   **139** Charles returned to Gascony,
     þer he duelled siker apliȝt.
     So he biheld opon a niȝt,
         Vp to þe firmament,   **142**
     A way of sterres he seiȝe y-wis,   and one night saw a line of stars
     Out of spaine in to galis,   pointing towards Galicia.
         As red as brond þat brent.   **145**
     He bi-souȝt god in trinite
     To sende him grace wite wat it be,
         Wiþ wel gode entent.   **148**

14   ¶ & in þe pouȝt þat he was in,
     þer com a voice, & spac to him,
         Wiþ a milde steuen,   **151** And the voice of James the Apostle,
     " Iames þe apostel bi crist,
     Iones broþer, þe wangelist,
         Godes deciple of heuen,   **154**
     þat god bad prechy on þe se,
     For þi herodes lete me sle,   whom Herod had killed,
         þer of y þe neuen,   **157**
     Mi body liþ in galis,   told him how his body lay in Galicia, seven days' journey away,
     Biȝond speyne for soþe y-wis,
         Jurnays mo þan seuen.   **160**

15   ¶ For þi me wondreþ wiþouten fail,
     þat þou comest nouȝt[1] to do batayl,   [1 written over the line.]
         þat lond for to winne,   **163**
     & ȝif þou winnes þat lond y-wis,   and that he was to go and rescue it ;
     Y schal þe bring in to þat blis,
         þer ich woni inne.   **166**
     Al þat me sekeþ more & lesse,
     Schal haue for-ȝeuenes   for which he should have for-giveness of all his sins.
         Of her dedeli sinne.   **169**
     Now wende & do as y þe sede,
     & in batayl þou schalt spede,
         When þou it will biginne.   **172**

The line of stars betokened that Charles should conquer all the country.

[fol. 264, col. 1.]

[1 MS. Iameis.]

Thrice did the vision appear,

and Charles started with a large army.

First he laid siege to Pampiloun for six months,

but could not win it.

Charles prays to God to enable him to win the city,

and immediately the walls fall down.

16 ¶ Þe way of sterres bitokneþ y-wis,
Þat of spaine & of galis
  Þou shalt be *conquerer*;   175
Lorain & lombardye,
Gascoyne, bayoun, & pikardye,
  Schal be in þi pouwer."   178
Þus com þe apostel Iames,[1]
Þries to charls, & seyd þis,
  Þat was so stoute & fer.   181
Now wendeþ charls wiþ his ost
Into speyne wiþ michel bost,
  As ȝe may forward here.   184

17 ¶ Þe first cite was pampiloun,
Þat was a swiþe noble toun,
  Þat charls gan asayl;   187
& sex moneþes he it bi-lay apliȝt,
Þat noþing winne he it no miȝt,
  For alle his batayle.   190
For þe walles so strong were,
He no miȝt haue non entre þere
  Wiþ outen ani fayl,   193
Þer were mani strong gines,
& fele þousand of sarazines,
  Swiþe heyȝe of parail.   196

18 ¶ Þan praid charls to god of heuen,
"Lord, he seyd, here mi steuen,
  Astow art ful of miȝt,   199
Sende me grace þis cite to winne,
& sle þe sarrazins her inne,
  Þat don oȝain þe riȝt."   202
Þo felle þe walles of þe cite,
Charls entred wiþ his meyne,
  Als a douhti kniȝt,   205
& þurch þe miracle þat was þere,
Ten þousand sarrazins cristned were,
  In þat ich niȝt.   208

19   ¶ & þo þat nold nouȝt cristned be,
    He lete hem hong opon a tre,
        Er he þennes pase.   211
    Þus charls þurch spayn gan gon,   Then Charles marched through-
    & wan þe cites eurichon,   out Spain,
        Al þurch godes grace.   214
    Where he com in ani erd,
    Ich man was of him aferd,
        þat loked on his face.   217
    þe names of eueri cite   and took every city :
    þat he wan, y schal tel ȝe
        Er ich hennes pase.   220

20   ¶ Visim, lameche, & sumy,   [fol. 264, col. 2.]
    Colomuber, luche, & vrry,
        Brakare & vimaraile,   223
    *Com*postel, a cite grete,   amongst them Compostella,
    Aurilian & tullet,
        þat strong is to asayl ;   226
    Golddelfagar & salamencha,   Salamanca,
    Vline, canayls, madris, al swa   Madrid,
        Calatorie & lestoyl,   229
    Medinacel, an heiȝe cite,
    Segouus þe grete, & salamenche,   Segovia,
        Gramie & sturgel,   232

21   ¶ Godian & emerite,   Godian,
    Bourg *in* spaine, þᵗ nis nouȝt lite,
        A swiþe noble toun ;   235
    Nasers & maþed,
    Carion & vrpaled,
        & oche of gret renoun ;   238 Oche,
    Burbagalle, a castel al so,
    Costant, petros, & oþ*er* mo,
        Bayet & pampiloun,   241 Pampiloun,
    Ventos *in* þe grene vale,
    Caparre, eustorge, & entale,
        Gascoine & bayoun,   244 Bayonne,

22 ¶ Toutor, a strong castel,

Portugal and
Landulif & portingal,

Saragossa,
     Burnam & saragouns,   247

Granada,
Granad & satyne,

Costaunce & deine,
     Teragon & valouns,   250

Seville, Acon,
Leride, acoun, & siuile,

Charls wan in a while,
     Agabie & vrens,   253

and many others.
Quaramelide, gibalderie,

Barbaster, vice, & almarie,
     Agabie & sisens.   256

At Acon lay
Torquas, the dis-
ciple of St. James,
23 ¶ Acoun, þat y spak of ere,

Seyn Iames deciple liþ þere,
     þat hat seyn torquas ;   259

A swiþe fair oliif tre

Beside his toumbe men may se,
     þat springeþ þurch godes grace ;   262

at whose tomb
many miracles
were wrought.
Opon his fest in mid may,

þer on is front of gret noblay,

[fol. 264, back,
col. 1.]
     Boþe more & lasse ;   265

& who þat sekeþ hem verrament,

At þe day of iuggement,
     Schal se godes face.   268

The whole of
Spain did Charles
win,
24 Alle þe londes þat were in spayne,
    Wiþ dint of swerd wan charlmain,
     Portingale & lauers ;   271

Landuluf & chastel,

Bigairs, bastles, & londes fele,
     Moys & nauers.   274

Alle þe londes he wan ȝern,

till he came to
Lucerne, which
Til he com to lucern,
     So stout he was & fers,   277

withstood him a
whole year.
& tvelmoneþ he it bilay apliȝt,

& noþing win he it miȝt,
     For al his dusse-pers.   280

25   ¶ þo preyd charls to god aboue,
   þat he him sent grace sone,
      þe cite for to winne.   283
   þo fel þe walles adoun riȝtes,
   King charls entred wiþ his kniȝtes,
      þurch þat ich ginne ;   286
   Charls acurssed þat cite,
   & ventos, & caparre, & deneye,
      For her dedeli sinne ;   289
   Deserd þai were after þan,
   þat neuer seþþen no cristen man,
      No durst com þer inne.   292

26   ¶ For charls curssed þo lucern,
   Also tite þe toun ganbern,
      & schal don euer mo ;   295
   & of þe smoc of þat toun,
   Mani takeþ þer of pusesoun,
      & dyeþ in michel wo :   298
   & þer þe oþer þre cites stode,
   Beþ waters red of helle flode,
      & fisches ther in al blo ;   301
   & who þat wil nouȝt leue me,
   In spaine men may þe soþe y-se,
      Who þat wil þider go.   304

27   ¶ & while charls was in þat stede,
   A fair miracle god for him dede,
      Er he gan þennes wende ; 307
   Braunches of vines charls sett,
   In marche moneþ wiþ outen lett,
      As was þe riȝt kende ;   310
   & amorwe grapes þai bere,
   Red & ripe to kerue þere,
      For paners þai gun sende ; 313
   And for paners þai crid þo,
   Ȝete men clepeþ þe cite so,
      & schal to þe warldes ende. 316

Marginal glosses:

Then prayed Charles again,

and again the walls fell down.

And Charles cursed that town and others,

so that none could live in them,

and the waters became red like hell-flood, and the fishes black, as you may see to this day.

And God showed Charles a miracle,

[fol. 264, back, col. 2.] for in March the vines bare ripe grapes, more than they could carry.

<table>
<tr><td>All the towns in Spain Charles won back,</td><td>28</td><td>¶ Clodonius þe first cristen king,
& clotayrs wiþ outen lesing,
  King dagabers & pipin,
Won mani tounes in spaine,
Ac þe gode charlmain,
  Wan it al wiþ gin :</td><td>

319

322</td></tr>
<tr><td>and destroyed all the Saracen's idols.</td><td></td><td>Alle þe maumetes in spaine were,
þat were þe sarrazins leue & dere,
  King charls & turpin,
þai destroyd þurch godes miȝt,
Sum þurch miracle & sum þurch fiȝt,
  So seyt þe latin.</td><td>

325

328</td></tr>
<tr><td>A statue had Mahoun made with great craft,</td><td>29</td><td>¶ & an image of gret pouste,
Stode on a roche bi þe se,
  In þe gilden lond ;
His name was salanicodus,
As a man y-schapen he wes,
  & held a glaive an hond,</td><td>

331

334</td></tr>
<tr><td>and in it put many fiends to protect it,</td><td></td><td>Mahoun maked him wiþ gin,
& dede mani fendes þer in,
  As ich vnderstond,
For to susten þe ymage,
& sett him on heiȝe stage,
  For no man nold he wond.</td><td>

337

340</td></tr>
<tr><td></td><td>30</td><td>¶ þe face of him was turned souþe riȝt,
In her lay the sarrazins founde apliȝt
  Of iubiter & mahoun ;</td><td>

343</td></tr>
<tr><td>for that statue would fall when a king brought Spain to Christianity.</td><td></td><td>þat when y-born were þe king,
þat schuld spaine to cristen bring,
  þe ymage schuld falle adoun ;</td><td>

346</td></tr>
<tr><td>Charles overthrew that statue,</td><td></td><td>Charls dede þat ymage falle,
& wan in spaine þe cites alle,
  Boþe tour & toun ;</td><td>

349</td></tr>
<tr><td>and with the spoils built churches.</td><td></td><td>& wiþ þe tresour þat he wan þere
Mani a chirche he lete arere,
  þat was of gret renoun.</td><td>

352</td></tr>
</table>

31 ¶ þe first chirche for soþ y-wis,
  Was seyn Iames in galis,
    þat he lete arere,   355
  Wiþ an hundred chanouns & her priour,
  Of seynt ysador þe confessour,
    For to serui þere :   358
  & in aise a chapel,
  Of lim & ston y-wrouȝt ful wel,
    Of werk riche & dere,   361
  & seyn Iames at burdewes,
  & on at tolous, anoþer at anevaus,
    & mo as ȝe may here.   364

First he built a church to St. James in Galicia,

and a chapel at Aix,

and churches at Bordeaux, Tolouse, and elsewhere.

[fol. 265, col. 1.]

32 Charls duelled siker apliȝt,
  þre mones & fourten niȝt,
    In bayoun wiþ his ost,   367
  þer fel a miracle of a kniȝt,
  Wiche þat was to deþ y-diȝt,
    þurch þe holy gost;   370
  Sir romain for soþe he hiȝt,
  Er he dyd he hadde his riȝt,
    Wiþ outen ani bost ;   373
  On of his frendes he cleped him to :
  " Y schal dye it is so,
    Ful wele þou it wost.   376

While Charles was at Bayonne,

a miracle happened to a knight,

Sir Romain.

33 ¶ Mine cloþes þat ichaue,
  þer wiþ þat y be brouȝt in graue,
    Wiþ mete & drink & liȝt,   379
  & sel min hors on heiȝeing
  Pouer clerkes sauters to sing,
    þer to þat it be diȝt ; "   382
  & when he hadde y-seyd þus stille,
  Also it was godes wille,
    þan died þe kniȝt,   385
  þe hors was seld wiþ outen duelinges,
  For to hundred schillinges,
    & put it vp apliȝt.   388

On his death-bed he bequeathed his horse to be sold and the money given to the church.

His executor sold it for two hundred shillings, and kept the money.

34   ¶ & at þe nende of þritti niȝt,

To his seketour com þe ded kniȝt,

     & seyd in þis maner :   391

"Mi soule is in heuen blis,

For þe loue of min almis,

     þat y sett here ;   394

& for þou hast at-hold min,

þritti days ichaue ben *in* pin,

     þat wel strong were,   397

Paradis is graunted me,

& in þat pain þou schalt be,

     þat ich was in ere."   400

35   ¶ þe ded þus in his way went,

& he awaked verrament,

     & wonder hadde apliȝt ;   403

& amorwe his sweuen he told,

To erls & to barouns bold,

     To squiers & to kniȝt :   406

& amonges hem alle,

As þai stoden in þe halle,

     þer com a windes fliȝt,   409

& fele fendes þ^t were swift,

& beren him vp in to þe lift,

     & held hi*m* þere four niȝt.   412

36   ¶ Seriau*n*ce þe bodi souȝt,

Ac þai no miȝt it finde nouȝt,

     Four dayes no more.   415

Fro bayoun he went wiþ his ost,

& þurch nauern wiþ miche bost,

     þe bodi þai founde þore,   418

þer þe fendes had let hi*m* felle,

& bere his soule in to helle,

     To hard paines sore.   421

So schal eueri sekatour,

þe dedes gode abigge wel sour,

     þat hye bi-nimeþ þe pore.   424

37 No[w] late we be of þis þing,
   & speke of charles þe king,
     þat michel was of miȝt, 427
Of his lengþe & his brede,
As þe latin ous sede,
     Ichil ȝou rede ariȝt ; 430
Tventi fete he was o lengþe,
& al so of gret strengþe,
     & of a stern sight, 433
Blac of here & rede of face,
Whare he com in ani place,
     He was a douhti kniȝt. 436

Now will I tell you of Charles.

He was 20 feet in height,

with black hair and a ruddy complexion.

38 ¶ Four times in þe ȝere,
On his heued he bere,
     þe holy croun of þorn, 439
At ester, at wissontide,
& at seyn iames day wiþ pride,
     & in ȝole as god was born. 442
& atte þe mete in þe halle,
Among his kniȝtes alle,
     A drawe swerd him biforn, 445
þis was þe maner ay,
& schal be til domesday,
     Of emperour y-corn. 448

Four times in the year,

at Easter, Whitsuntide, [fol. 265, back. col. 1.] St. James's day and Christmas, he wore at his table the holy crown of thorns.

39 ¶ & whare he slepe aniȝt,
Wel wise he was & wiȝt,
     & douted of tresoun, 451
An hundred kniȝtes him kept,
þat non of hem no slept,
     þat were of gret renoun, 454
& eueri duȝti kniȝt
Held a torche liȝt,
     & a naked fauchoun. 457
þus king charls lay,
Wiþ his ost mani a dai,
     In þe cite of pampiloun. 460

When he slept 100 knights guarded him,

each with a torch and a drawn sword.

One day came tidings to Charles of a doughty knight called

40 ¶ & on a day com tiding,
Vnto charls the king,
    Al of a douhti kniȝt,   463
Was comen to nasers :
Stout he was & fers,

Vernagu,

    Vernagu he hiȝt ;   466
Of babiloun þe soudan
þider him sende gan,

who had come to fight with him.

    Wiþ king charls to fiȝt,   469
So hard he was to fond,
þat no dint of brond,
    No greued him apliȝt.   472

41 ¶ He hadde tventi men strengþe,
& fourti fet of lengþe,

He was 40 feet in height;

    þilke panim hede,   475

his face 4 feet across,

& four fet in þe face,
Y-meten in þe place,

and his shoulders 15 feet.

    & fiften in brede,   478
His nose was a fot & more,
His browe as brestles wore,
    He þat it seiȝe it sede,   481

He was a loath-some sight and as black as pitch.

He loked loþeliche,
& was swart as piche,
    Of him men miȝt adrede.   484

[fol. 265, back, col. 2.] He challenged Charles or any of his knights to fight.

42 Charls com to nasers
  Wiþ his dusse pers,
    To se þat painim.   487
He asked wiþ outen fayl,
Of king charls batayl,
    To fiȝt oȝaines him :   490

Charles was astonished,

Charls wonderd þo,
When he seiȝe him go,
    He bi-held him ich alim,   493
For seþþen he was y-bore,
He no hadde y-sen bifore,

for never had he seen any so grim.

    Non þat was so grim.   496

43 ¶ Sir oger þe danais,
A kniȝt ful curtays,
    To him first was y-sent;   499
& at his coming,
Vernagu an heyȝeing,
    Vnder his arm hi*m* hent,   502
Y-armed as he was,
He toke him in þe plas,
    & to þe castel he went :·   505
Sir oger schamed sore,
Him o-þouȝt þat com þore,
    & held him foule y-schent.   508

44 ¶ Reynald de aubeþpine
Was sent to þat sarrazin,
    He serued him al so ;   511
& seyd to charlmain,
"Sir, þo þou won spain,
    Hadestow non better þo?   514
So mahoun me ȝiue rest,
Oȝain ten swiche þe best,
    To fiȝt ich wold go."   517
Sir costentin of rome,
& þerl of nauntes come,
    To fiȝt wiþ boþe to.   520

45 ¶ & vernagu bar boþe,
No were þai neuer so wroþe,
    To nassers castel,   523
Vnder aiþer arm on,
As stille as ani ston,
    Miȝt þai nouȝt wiþ hi*m* mele.   526
Þo charls sent ten,
Al so he serued his men,
    Miȝt no man wiþ hi*m* dele.   529
Charls bi-þouȝt þo,
Ȝif he sent mo,
    It were him wroþer hele.   532

Ogier first essayed,

but Vernagu took him under his arm,

and walked off with him.

Reynald was the next,

but he was served in the same way.

After him Costentin and the Earl of Nantes came out at once,

but Vernagu carried them off,

one under each arm.

Then Charles sent 10 at once, but they all were treated in the [fol. 266, col. 1.] same way.

46 R oland þe gode kniȝt,
    þo bad leue to fiȝt,
      Oȝain þat painim,   535
King charls seyd, " nay,
þou no schalt nouȝt bi þis day,
      He is to stout & grim."   538
So long he him bad,

þat leue of him he hadde.
      Rouland armed him,   541
& com anon riȝt
In to þe feld, to fiȝt
      Oȝain þat sarrazin.   544

47 ¶ & at his coming þare,
Sir vernagu was ware

      & tok him vnder his hond,   547
Out of his sadel he gan him bere,
& on his hors swere
      He set roulond :   550

& rouland smot him so,
þat vernagu þo
      Vnto þe grounde wond.   553
& when þe cristen seiȝe þis,
þat vernagu fallen is,
      þai þonked godes sond.   556

48 ¶ þai lopen opon her stede,

& swerdes out þai brede,
      & fiȝt þai gun þo.   559
Rouland wiþ durindale,

Brewe him miche bale,
      & carf his hors ato :   562
When vernagu was o fot,
He no couþe no better bot,
      To rouland he gan go,   565

In þe heued he smot his stede,
þat ded to grounde he ȝede,
      O fot þan were þai bo.   568

49 ¶ A fot þai tok þe fiȝt,
   & vernagu a non riȝt,
      His swerd he had y-lore.   571

   Rouland wiþ al his miȝt,
   He stired him as a kniȝt,   *[fol. 266, col. 2]*
      & yaf him dintes sore.   574

   Til it was ogaiṅ þe none,
   þus þai layd opon,
      Ay til þai weri wore :   577

   Douk rouland sone he fond,
   þat wiþ no dint of brond,
      He slouȝ him neuer more.   580

50 ¶ When it com to þe neue,
   Vernagu bad leue,
      To resten of þat fiȝt :   583

   Rouland him trewþe ȝaf,
   So he most bring a staf,
      After his wil y-diȝt ;   586

   Vernagu graunted wel
   & went to her hostel
      When þat was niȝt.   589

   Amorwe wiþ outen fail,
   þai com to þe batayl,
      Aiþer as douhti kniȝt.   592

51 ¶ Sir rouland brouȝt a staf
   þat king charls him ȝaf,
      þat was long & newe,   595

   þe bodi of a ȝong oke,
   To ȝif þer-wiþ a stroke,
      He was touȝ & trewe.   598

   & wiþ þat gode staf,
   Wel mani dintes he ȝaf
      Vernagu þe schrewe.   601

   & at þe non apliȝt,
   þai gun anoþer fiȝt,
      & stones to gider þrewe.   604

Marginal glosses:
- They fought on foot,
- but Roland could not hurt him with a sword.
- At even Vernagu proposed to adjourn the fight till the next day.
- Roland agreed on condition that he might bring a staff as his arm.
- So next day he brought a young oak,
- with which he belaboured Vernagu.
- Then they took to stones.

52 ¶ Gode rappes for þe nones,
þai ȝauen wiþ þe stones,
  þat sete swiþe sore ;   607

þat helme & heye targe,
þurch her strokes large,
  þer wiþ þai broken wore.   610

& vernagu at þat cas,
So sore asleped was,
  He no miȝt fiȝt no more :   613
At rouland leue he toke,
þat time, so seyt þe boke,
  For to slepe þore.   616

53 ¶ Roland ȝaf leue him,
For to slepe wele afin,
  & rest him in þat stounde, 619

& seyd þat he nold,
For þe cite ful of gold
  Be þer wiþ y-founde,   622
Slepeand to slen a kniȝt,
þei þat he had in fiȝt,
  ȝif him deþes wounde.   625

þo vernagu lay adoun,
To slepe he was boun,
  þere opon þe grounde.   628

54 ¶ & vernagu rout þore,
As a wild bore,
  þo he on slepe was :   631

To him rouland gan gon,
& tok þe gretest ston
  þat lay in þat place,   634
He leyd vnder his heued y-wis
For him þouȝt it lay amis,
  To lowe at þat cas.   637
& vernagu vp stode,
He stard as he were wode,
  When he awaked was,   640

55   ¶ Vernagu asked anon,
      "Who leyd þis gret ston,
           Vnder min heued so?   643
      It no miȝt neuer be,
      Bot ȝif he were a kniȝt fre.
           Wist ich who it were,   646
      He schuld be me leue & dere,
           [*No gap in the MS.*]
           þei þat he were mi fo."   649
      Quaþ rouland, sikerly,
      "Certes it was y,
           For þat þou rot so.   652

56   ¶ & when þo me louest miche,
      Now tel me sikerliche,
           Whi þou art so hard,   655
      þat no þing may þe dere,
      Knif, no ax, no spere,
           No no dint of sward."   658
      Quaþ vernagu sikerly,
      "No man is harder þan y,
           Fram þe nauel vp ward,   661
      For-þi y com hider y-wis,
      To fiȝt wiþ king charlis,
           Wiþ þe hore bard."   664

57   ¶ Vernagu to rouland sede,
      "Al so þi god þe spede,
           Whare were þou y-born?"   667
      "In fraunce, bi seynt austin,
      King charls cosyn,
           Our kinde lord y-corn.   670
      We leueþ opon ihū,
      þat is ful of vertu,
           þat bare þe croun of þorn.   673
      & ȝe leueþ in þe fende,
      For-þi wiþ outen ende,
           ȝe schul be for lorn."   676

Marginal glosses:
Vernagu wondered greatly at this act of courtesy,
and asked who did it.
Roland asked the Saracen how it was he could not hurt him.
Vernagu told him that only in the navel was he vulnerable.
[fol. 266, back, col. 2]
"Where wert thou born?" asked Vernagu.
Roland told him,
and how he was a believer in Jesus Christ.

58 ¶ & when þat vernagu
Y-herd speke of ihū,
  He asked wat man he was. 679

Roland answered,
" The king of
Paradise,

Sir rouland seyd, " he is
þe king of paradys,
  & lord ful of gras, 682

who was born of a
virgin,

In a maiden he was bore,
To bigge þat was forlore,
  As sonne passeþ þurch þe glas, 685

suffered for man-
kind on the cross,

& dyed opon þe rode,
For our alder gode,
  & nouȝt for his gilt it nas : 688

59 ¶ & suffred woundes fiue,
& ros fram ded to liue,
  þan þridde day ; 691

rose on the third
day from death to
life,

& fet out adam & eue,
& mo þat were him leue,
  Fram helle for soþe to say, 694

and ascended into
heaven, one God
in Three
Persons."

& sitt in trinite,
O god in persones thre;
  Swiche is our lay." 697

¶ Vernagu seyd þo,
" It no miȝt neuer be so,
  þer of y sigge nay. 700

" How could he be
one and three ? "
asked Vernagu.

60 ¶ Hou miȝt it euer be,
þat he were on & thre ?
  Tel me now þe skille." 703

Rouland þan sede,
" Al so god me spede,
  ȝis wiþ a gode wille. 706

[fol. 267, col. 1]
Roland answers :
" As in a harp are
three things,
wood, and strings,
and sound, so in
God are three
persons :

As þe harp has þre þinges,
Wode & soun & strenges,
  & mirþe is þer tille, 709

So is god persones þre,
& holeliche on in vnite,
  Al þing to ful-fille. 712

61   ¶ & as þe sonne haþ þinges þre,
     Hete & white on to se,
         & is ful of liȝt,   715
     So is god in trinite,
     Vnite & mageste,
         & lord ful of miȝt."   718
     Quaþ vernagu, "now y se,
     Hou he is god in persones þre,
         Now ich wot þat riȝt,   721
     Ac hou þat he bicom man,
     The lord þat þis world wan,
         þer of no haue y no siȝt."   724

And as in the sun are heat, brightness, and light, so is the Trinity in Unity."

"Now I understand," said Vernagu; "but how could God become man ?"

62   ¶ Quaþ rouland, "he þat ous bouȝt,
     & al þing maked of nouȝt,
         Wele miȝt he be so hende,   727
     þat he wald sende his sone,
     In a maiden for to wone,
         Wiþ outen mannes kende."   730
     Quaþ vernagu, "saunfayl,
     þer of ichaue gret meruail,
         Hou miȝt he fram hir wende,   733
     Hou miȝt he of hir be bore,
     þat was a maiden bi fore,
         Y no may nouȝt haue in mende."   736

"God," said Roland, "who is Almighty, sent His Son to be born man of a Virgin ?"

"How could a Virgin bear a child ?" asked Vernagu.

63   ¶ Rouland seyd to vernagu,
     "Mi lordes fader ihū,
         Is so michel of miȝt,   739
     þat he made sonne & se,
     & fisches in þe flod to be,
         Boþe daye & niȝt :   742
     Wele may he þan, as y þe er seyd,
     Ben y-bore of a maide,
         Wiþ outen wem apliȝt."   745
     Quaþ vernagu, "it may wele be,
     Ac hou he dyed y no can nouȝt se,
         Tel me now þat riȝt.   748

"God, who made sun and sea, night and day, could easily do that," replied Roland.

"That might well be," said Vernagu; "but how could God die,

64 ¶ For i nist neuer no man,
þat aros after þan,
   When þat he ded was,   751
& ȝif he godes sone were,
He no miȝt nouȝt dye þere :
   Tel me now þat cas."   754

Quaþ rouland, " y schal tel þe.
His bodi slepe vpon þe tre,
   & þe þridde day aras,   757
His godhed waked euer & ay,
& to helle tok þe way,
   & bond satanas.   760

65 ¶ So schul we al arise,
& of þe dome agrise,
   Atte day of iuggement,   763
& answerey for our dede,
þe gode & þe quede,
   Hou we our liif haue spent."   766

Quaþ vernagu, "now ichot wel,
Hou he aros ichadel,
   & haue in min entent   769
Ac hou he steyȝe to heuen,
Y no can nouȝt neuen,
   No wite verrament."   772

66 ¶ þan seyd rouland,
"O vernagu, vnderstand,
   Herken now to me.   775
þat ich lord þat wiþ his miȝt,
In a maiden a-liȝt,
   Y-born for to be,   778
As þe sonne aros in þe est,
& decended in þe west,
   Astow miȝt now se,   781
Riȝt so dede god almiȝt,
Mounted in to heuen liȝt,
   & sit in trinite."   784

67 ¶ Quaþ vernagu, "now ich wot,
Ӡour cristen lawe eueri grot,
    Now we wil fiӡt.
Wheþer lawe better be,
Sone we schul y-se,
    Long ar it be niӡt."
Rouland a dint him ӡaf,
Wiþ his gode staf,
    þat he kneled apliӡt,
& vernagu to him smot,
& carf his staf fot hot,
    Euen ato ariӡt.

787 "Now," said Vernagu, "I understand your religion every whit: let us try whose religion God will prevail."

790

793 They then resumed their fight, [fol. 267, back, col. 1] and Vernagu cut Roland's staff in two.

796

68 ¶ þo rouland kneld adoun,
& maked an orisoun,
    To god in heuen liӡt,
& seyd, "lord vnder stond
Y no fiӡt for no lond,
    Bot for to saue þi riӡt,
Sende me now miӡt & grace,
Here in þis ich place,
    To sle þat foule wiӡt."
An angel com ful sone,
& seyd "herd is þi bone,
    Arise rouland & fiӡt,

799 Roland fell on his knees, and prayed God for help to overcome the Saracen.

802

805

An angel soon appeared, and bade him arise,

808

69 ¶ & sched þe schrewes blod,
For he nas neuer gode,
    Bi lond no bi se :
þei alle prechours aliue,
To cristen wald him schriue,
    Gode nold be neuer be."
When rouland herd þat steuen,
He stirt him vp ful euen,
    & fauӡt wiþ hert fre ;
Strokes bi sex & seuen,
Togider þis kniӡtes ӡeuen
    þat mani man miӡt y-se.

and slay the infidel.

811

814

Roland started up, and laid on strokes by six and seven.

817

820

70 ¶ Rouland wiþ outen dueling,
þurch miȝt of heuen king,
    Vernagu he smot,   823
þat þe left arm, & þe scheld
Fel forþ in to þe feld,
    Fram þat painim fot hot :   826
His arm þo he had lore,
Swiþe wo him was *þer* fore
    & fast he fauȝt y wot.   829

He smot rouland on þe croun,
A strok wiþ his fauchoun,
    þat þurch þe helme it bot.   832

71 ¶ No hadde ben þe bacinet,
þat þe strok wiþ sett,
    Rouland hadde ben aqueld.   835
þe sarrazin sayd aswiþe,
" Smite ich eft on siþe

    þi liif is bouȝt & seld."   838
Rouland answerd, " nay,
Mine worþ þe raþer pay,
    Bi god þat al þing weld ;"   841

& wiþ a strok ful large,
He clef þe sarrazins targe,
    þat half fel in þe feld.   844

72 ¶ & at anoþer venov,
Roland smot vernagu,
    þat he fel doun to grounde,   847
& rouland wiþ durindale
ȝaf him strokes fale,
    & his deþes wounde.   850
þe paynem crid, " help, mahoun,
& Iubiter of gret renoun,
    þat beþ so michel of mounde,   853

As ȝe beþ miȝt-ful helpeþ me,
þat ich miȝt y-venged me
    Of þis cristen hounde."   856

73 ¶ Rouland louȝ for þat cri,
& syd, "mahoun, fikerly,
    No may þe help nouȝt :   859
No Iubiter, no apolin,
No is worþ þe brust of a swin,
    In hert no in þouȝt."   862
His ventail he gan vn-lace,
& smot of his heued in þe place,
    & to charls it brouȝt :   865
þo þonked he god in heuen,
& mari wiþ milde steuen,
    þat he so hadde y-wrouȝt.   868

74 ¶ & al þe folk of þe lond,
For onour of roulond,
    þonked god old & ȝong :   871
& ȝede a procesioun,
Wiþ croice & gomfaynoun,
    & salue miri song,   874
Boþe widowe & wiif in place,
þus þonked godes grace,
    Alle þo þat speke wiþ tong.   877
To otuel also ȝern,
þat was a sarrazin stern,
    Ful sone þis word sprong.   880

The Romance of Otuel.

Otuel.

[*The numbers in brackets in the margin refer to the
corresponding lines of "Roland and Otuel."*]

1   Erkneþ boþe ȝinge & olde,
    þat willen heren of batailles bolde,
    & ȝe wolle a while duelle,
    Of bolde batailles ich wole ȝou telle, 4
    þat was sumtime bitwene
  Cristine men & sarrazins kene.

*Hearken all,
young and old,*

*and I will tell you
of the wars
between the
Christians and
Saracens.*

2 ¶ þere was sumtime a king in *france*,
    A douȝty man wiþ spere & launce, 8
    & made sarazins ful tame,
    King charles was his name,
    & was born in seint denys,
    Nouȝt bote a litel fram parys, 12
    & was a wol treu kniȝt,
    & meintenede cristendom ariȝt.

*Once there was a
doughty king of
France, Charles, a
true knight,*

3 ¶ In his time, a king þer was,
    An heþene þat vncristned was, 16
    þat was king of lumbardie,
    & was y-hoten king garsie.
    Marsile was his al so,
    & manie oþer londes mo. 20
    A swiþe gret lord he was,
    In his time non suych þer nas,
    On ihū crist ne leuede he nouȝt,
    þat him hadde so dere a-bouȝt. 24
    He leuede al in maumettrie,
    & for-sok god & seinte marie.
    In alle londes þere he wente,
    He slouȝ al þat euere he hente, 28

*in whose time was
a heathen king of
Lombardy,*

named Garsie.

*A great lord he
was,*

*but he believed
not on Jesus
Christ,*

and his whole
thought was to
destroy Christi-
anity.

þat wolde on ihū crist bileue,
& tok þe lond to his byheue :
Niȝt & day it was his þout,
To bringe cristendom to nout.   32

Never in all
heathendom was
there so great a
king :
[fol. 268, col. 2]

4   ¶ In heþenesse þer nas no king,
þat ne hel[d] of him sum þing,
Or dude him omage or feute.
Suich a miȝty king was he,   36
Alle þei scholden to him bouwe.
He was lord of londes ynowe,
& ȝit he þouȝte wit maistrie,
Habben al cristendom to gye :   40
Al cristendom more & lasse,
He þouȝte to maken heþennesse.

when he held his
parliament,

5   ¶ Whan he wolde hauen a *parlement*,
þere com to his comaundeme*n*t,   44
To helpen hym wit alle þinges,
Fiftene heþene kinges :

fifteen kings came
at his command,
and swore to join
in war on
Charles,

& alle þei were togidere sworn,
þat cristendom scholde be lorn,   48
& maden alle here ordenau*n*ce,
To werren uppon þe king of F*r*ance,
For þei herden alle tidinges,

for he was the
greatest of Chris-
tian kings.

þat he was chef of cristene gynges,   52
& þe king wiste it wel.
Nou schulle ȝe here hou it bifel,

On Childermas-
day Charles with
his douze-peres
went towards
Paris.

6   ¶ Hit was on childermasse day,
Soþ to segge wiþ outen nay,   56
þat king charles of sein denys,
Wente him to ward parys.   [39.]
Hise duzze peres wit him he na*m*,
& muche poeple to him kam,   60
& token alle here consail þare,
þat þei wolden wiþ alle fare,

Into Marsile riden and gon, [46]
& werren þere wiþ godes foon, 64
& hadden set a certein day,
To wenden þider wiþ outen delay : On his way he heard of a doughty Saracen,
Bote ar þei þiderward ferden,
Suiche tydinges þei herden, 68
Of a sarasin[1] douȝti & good,
þat a-moeuede al here blod.

7 ¶ þer com a sarazin ful of rage, [55]
Fram king garsie in message, 72
In to paris þe wei he nam,
& to þe kinges paleis he kam.
Otuwel his name was, named Otuel,
Of no man a-fered he nas, 76
Into þe paleis þo he cam,[2]
A skwier be þe hon[d] he nam, [fol. 268, back, col. 1.]
& seide : "ich am comen her,
Kyng garsies messager, 80 who was sent as a messenger from Garsie, to Charles
To speke wiþ charles, king of þis lond,
& wiþ a kniȝt þat heet Roulond, Roland,
& a noþer hatte oliuer, and Oliver.
Kniȝtes holden wiþouten peer : 84
þose þre ich biseche þe,
þat þou telle me whiche þei be."

8 ¶ þe skwier þouȝte wel by siȝt, Otuel is led by a squire into
þat Otuwel was a douȝti kniȝt, 88 Charles' presence
& for he was in message come,
Bi þe hond he haueþ him nome,
& ladde him in to þe halle,
Among þe grete lordes alle, 92
& þere þei stoden oppon her feet.
He schewede him where þe king seet,

[1] MS. sazasin.
[2] This line is twice written in the MS. ; at the end of fol. 268, col. 2, as above, and at the beginning of p. 268 back, col. 1, In to þe palais þo he cam.

& tauȝte him hou he scholde knowe,
þere þei seten oppon a rowe,   96
Roulond & olyuer,
& þe godde kniȝt ogger.

He went directly
up to Charles,

9 ¶ Anon as otuwel hadde a siȝt
Of charles þat was king & kniȝt,   100
For eye of no man he ne leet,
Bote wente to him þere he seet.

without any fear,

Hit was þe boldeste sarazin,
þat euere þorte drinke win,   104
& þat was sene wiþ oute lesing.
þo he spak wiþ charles þe king.

and said before
them all:
"Garsie, my lord,
defies thee, and
curses thee!"

He seide to him amydde his halle :   [93]
"Sire king, foule mote þe falle,   108
þou art a-boute for to greue
Mahoun þat we onne byleue,
þere fore haue þou maugre,
So þe greteþ garsie bi me,   112
þat me haueþ in message sent,
To seggen his comaundement.

And Roland
he challenged
to meet him in
the field in single
combat.

& þou, Roulond, þat art his kniȝt,   [109]
Nou ich knowe þe be siȝt,   116
May ich mete þe in þe feeld,
Wiþ þi spere & wiþ þi scheld,
Ich wole wyte, so mote Ich þe,
Riȝt bytwene me & te."[1]   120

[fol. 268, back,
col. 2.]
.   .   .   .   .   .
.   .   .   .   .   .
.   .   .   .   .   .
.   .   .   .   .   .
.   .   .   .   .   .
.   .   .   .   .   .

[1] (Eight lines lost in consequence of the cutting out of the illumination at the beginning of the poem. These eight lines were on the back of the illumination.)

10 ¶ .   .   .   .   .

   .   .   .   .   .

   " þat þou makest offe þis bost,
   Tel me nou ȝef þou wost."   [133]
   Quaþ otuwel, " so mote ich þe,   Said Otuel,
   I nelle nouȝt hele for eie of þe.   124 "I will tell thee.
   It was oppon a weddenesdai,   It was in April
   In aueril be-fore þe may,   that Garsie with
                                            20,000 men came
   King garsie þe weie nam,   to Rome,
   To þe Cite of rome he cam,   128
   Twenti þousende was þe sawe,
   þat were þare of sarazin lawe :
   Corsouse m[i swerde ful] harde fel,   where with my
                                           sword I slew full
   & bot þere Freinche flechs fol wel." 132 many
                                           Frenchmen."

11 ¶ Estuȝt of leggers, a freinshe kniȝt, Estut, a French
   He sterte op anon riȝt,   knight,
                                            aims a stroke at
   & kypte anon in his hond   Otuel with a
   A gret muche fir brond,   [155] 136 brand,
   & to otuwel a strok hadde ment,
   & Roulond by-nam him þe dent.   but Roland
                                            warded it off.

12 ¶ þanne seide charles þe king,
   " Ich for bede oppon alle þing,   140 Charles also
                                            interposed to
   þat noman be so wood,   protect him,
   For to don hym oþer þan good,
   A kinges messager for he is,
   He ne schal habbe non harm, i-wis." 144

13 ¶ " Sire king," quaþ otuwel, " be mi blod, but Otuel defies
                                                them all.
   & ani of hem be so wod,
   To drawe to me swerd or knif,
   Certes he schal lesen his lif."   148

14 ¶ þe kinges kniȝtes hadden tene,   The French
   Of otuwel wordes kene ;   knights are
                                           enraged,
   Wiþ þat word anon riȝt,
   Op starte a freinsche kniȝt,   152
   Bihinden otuwel he cam,

& be þe hod otuwel nam, [165

& braid wiþ so gret miȝt,

& braid adon þat heþene kniȝt, 156

& anon out wiþ a knif,

& wolde haue reued him his lif,

& þat sarazin otuwel,

Was i-armed swiþe wel, 160

þat he ne dede him nouȝt bote good,

Ne drouȝ of his bodi no blood.

15 ¶ He starte op & was wroþ,

To ligge longe him was loþ, 164

& Corsouze his brond he drouȝ, [175]

& þe kinges kniȝt he slouȝ,

& amang hem alle he stood,

& lokede as he were wood. 168

þe kinges kniȝtes were agramed,

& summe of hem were aschamed,

þat otuwel in þe halle,

Slouȝ a kniȝt among hem alle, 172

& bi-gunnen op to stonden,

& þouȝte to leggen on him honden.

16 ¶ Otuwel þer of was war,

& in his herte it him bar, 176

þat þei nere a-boute no good,

& seide to hem þere he stod ;

" Bi þe louerd fire mahoun, [179]

Kniȝtes i rede ȝe sitten a-doun. 180

For ȝef ani of ȝou so hardi be,

þat any strok munteþ to me,

Mahoun mi god ich here for-sake

Ȝef he sschal euere ordres take, 184

Of ani oþer bisschopes hond,

Bot of Corsouze mi gode brond."

17 þei be-helden otuwel alle,

Kniȝtes & skwieres in þe halle, 188

þer nas non þat þere stood,
þat ne wende otuel were wod,
& euere he held his swerd y-drawe,
& ȝaf nouȝt of hem alle an hawe.   192
King charles stood vpriȝt,
& comaundede a non riȝt,
þat no man sscholde be so wod,   [181]
To do þe messager nouȝt bote good.   196

18   ¶ Kniȝtes & sweines in þe halle,
Were wol glade þer of alle,
þat þe king so bad,
For mani of hem was sore adrad,   200
& þei wiþ drowen hem echone,
& euere stod otuwel al one,
& biheld hem as þei ȝede,
Ȝef ani him wolde strok dede.   204

19   ¶ þanne seide charles þe king :
" Bi god þat made alle þing,   [182]
Sarasin, nere þou messager,
Wroþer hele come þou her,   208
I rede þou ȝeld op þi brond,
& taket out of þin hond."

20   ¶ Quaþ otuwel, þat sarazin,
" Bi mahoun, þat is louerd myn,   212
I nelle take it out of min hond
To noman of al þi lond,
þat is þer inne geten & bore,
þat wind þou hauest ilore."   216

21   ¶ " Sarasin," quaþ roulond,
" Tak me þi swerd in myn hond,
& iche wole saue þe bi mi blod,
Sschal noman do þe nouȝt bote good,   220
& whan þou art redi to fare
For soþe þi swerd sschal be ȝare."   [191]

22   ¶ Quaþ otuwel þe sarazin ;

"Bi mahoun, þat is louerd min,   224
þauȝ ich hadde skwieres twelue,
Ich wole bere myn swerd mi selue.
Holte o roum ! ich wolde rede,
& þanne dostou a god dede."   228

23 ¶ "Sarazin," quaþ charles þe king,
"Let ben al þi þretning.
Tel me nou alle & some
In what message artou come."   232
Otuwel, þat noble kniȝt,
Answerede a non riȝt :
"Hider me sente king garsie,   [205]
Spaine is his, an[d] lumbardie,   236
& manye londes name-couþe,
þat i ne mai nouȝt nemne wiþ mouþe ;
Bi me he sente þe to segge,
þou sscholdest cristendom a-legge,   240
& maken þine men in eche toun,
For to leuen on fire mahoun,
& þou & alle þine barons bolde,
Of him ȝe sschulle ȝoure londes holde,   244
þanne miȝtou amenden ȝif þou wilt,
þat þou hauest mahoun agult :
&, certes, bote it so bi-falle,
Garsie wele ȝiue þine londes alle,   248
To olecent of esclauenye,
þe kinges sone of Ermenie,
þat haueþ his .o. douȝter to wif,
þat he loueþ as his lif ;   252
þous sschall all þi murþe a-doun,
Bote þou leue on sire mahoun."

24 ¶ þe duzze pieres answerede þo :   [253]
"Certes, while we moun ride & go,   256
Fraunse sschal he neuere ȝiue,

To noman while we moun liue.
Sire king, his wille nou þou wost,
Let asemblen al þin ost,   260 *and call on Charles to march at once against Garsie.*
& let vs upon garsie wenden,
Alle hise londes for to sschenden;
Of wordes þat he haueþ ispeke,
For soþe we reden you be a-wreke." [258] 264

25 ¶ " Certes, sire king," quaþ otuwel,   *"Certes," said Otuel to Charles, "these knights can yelp well, but do little,*
" þine freinsche kniȝtes kune ȝelpe wel,
& whan þei beþ to werre ibrouȝt,
þanne be þei riȝt nouȝt.   268

26 ¶ þauȝ þou bringe wiþ sscheld & spere
Al þat euere may wepene bere,
To werren vpon [k]ing garsie,
Certes alle þei sscholden deie.   272
& þou art king, & old kniȝt,   *and you yourself are old and feeble,*
& hauest iloren al þi miȝt,
& in þi ȝinkþe, tak god hede,   *and even when young you were no doughty knight."*
þou nere neuere douȝti of dede."   276

27 ¶ þo was þe king was a-gramed,   *They are all ashamed and annoyed at Otuel's insolence,*
& alle hise duzze peres asschamed,
þat otuwel, þat heþene kniȝt,
Tolde of hem alle so liȝt.   280

28 ¶ Roulond bi þe king stood,   [292]
& ameuede al his blod,
& seide in wraþþe a non riȝt,
To otuwel þat heþene kniȝt;   284
" To werren on garsie ȝef we fare,   *and Roland declares that if ever he meets Otuel in fight, he will show him what a French knight can do.*
In bataille, and i mete þe þare,
& i may mete þe ariȝt,
Bi ihū þat is ful of miȝt,   288
þou ne sschalt neuere after þat day,
Despice freinchs man, ȝef ich may."

[fol. 269, back, col. 2.]

Otuel laughs,

29 ¶ " Ou3," quaþ otuwel & lou3,
"Wherto makestou it so tou3,   292
To þrete me in anoþer lond,
Nam ich [nou3t] here at þin hond,   [303]

and says he is quite ready at any moment.

3ef þou hauest wille to fi3te,
Whan euere þou wolt let þe di3te,   296
& þou sschalt finde me redi di3t,
In þe feld to bide fi3t."

Roland accepts the challenge,

30 ¶ "Bi god," quaþ roulond, "ich wolde be 3are
Whan ich wiste to finde þe þare,   300
& euele mote he þriue & þe,
þat ferst failleþ of me & te."

31 ¶ "3e leue 3a," quaþ otuwel þo,
" Wheþer so failleþ of us two,   304

and Otuel proposes the next day for the duel.

Ich wole finde mahoun to borwe,
Ich wile be redi erliche to morwe."

32 ¶ Quaþ roulond, þar he stod on grounde,

Roland is willing,

"Selpe me gode." feere ifounde   308
Ri3t be fore þe kinges Eien,
þat alle þe kinges kni3tes seien,

and they plight their words to each other.

Eiþer oþer his trewþe pli3te,
Vppon morwen for to fi3te.   312

Charles is pleased with Otuel,

33 ¶ King charles stod al stille,
& biheld his gode wille,
& seide, "it is harm, iwis,
þat þou nost what follaut is ;   316

and declares that if he will be baptized he will make him a rich man,

3ef þou woldes follaut take,
& þine false godes for sake,
Iche wolle make the, so mote ihc þe,
& tou wille bleue wiþ me,   320
A riche man in mi lond,
þat ich wille sikere þe on hond."

34 ¶ Otuwel, þat hardi kni3t,
Answerde a non ri3t :   324

“ Cristes cors vppon his heued,
þat me radde such a red,
To forsake mi god mahun ;
I nelle nouȝt leue thi false sarmon.” 328

35 ¶ þauȝ otuwel speke outrage,
For he was comen on message,
King charles þat was heende and god,
Noble soffre him habbe nouȝt bote god, 332
Bote seide to him a non riȝt :
“ Be þou skwier, be þou kniȝt,
Tel me ȝef thi conseil is nome,
Of what linage þou art come.” 336

36 ¶ Otuwel answerde þis ;
“ A kinges sone ich am, iwis,
Soþ to segge & nouȝt to lye,
Ich am þe kinges cosin garsie, 340
Fernagu myn eem was,
þat neuere ouer-comen nas,
Sir roulond þi cosin him slouȝ,
þere fore wole rise wo inouȝ, 344
þere fore ich desire so moche,
To fiȝte wiþ roulond sikerliche.
Ich wille to morewen in þe day,
Awreken his deþ ȝef ich may, 348
Nou he haueþ iseid his sawe,
þat he ne mai him nouȝt wiþ drawe,
þat we schule boþe fiȝten ifeere.
Nou ich wille þat þou it here, 352
Min Emes deþ ich [wille] a-wreke,
Or myn herte sschal to-breke.”

37 ¶ King charle[s] gan to meuen his blod,
Bot naþeles he was hende & good, 356
& nolde for hise wordes heȝe,
Don otuel no vileinie.

Bote comau*n*dede a non a swein,
Gon sechen him his chau*m*berlein,   [321] 360
A ȝing kniȝt ant nouȝt old,
þat was wel norssched & bold;

& seide to him, " sire Reiner,
Tak here þis messeger,   364
& to his in saueliche him lede,
þat for no word ne for no dede,
þat he haueþ don & seid,
þat no*n* hond be on him leid ;   368
& loke that he be wel idiȝt,
& onoured als a kniȝt."

38   ¶ þe chamberlein a non dede,
Als þe king him hadde ibede,   372
& ladde him hom to his in ;
& whan he was icomen in,
He tok his leue the chamberlein,
& wente to þe king aȝein.   376
Littel slep þe king þat niȝt,
For ferd of roulant þat gode kniȝt
Of þe bataille he hadde inome,
Leste he were ouer-come,   380
For þe king hadde sein fol wel,
þe kuntenau*n*se of otuel :
þe king wiste wel a fin,
Hit was a bold sarazin,   384
For he sauȝ hit wel by siȝt,
þo he sauȝ him slen his kniȝt.

39   ¶ On morwe þo þe dai sprong,
& þe larke bi-gan hire song,   388
King charles wente to cherche,
Godes werkes for to werche.   [330]
Roulond, his cosin, wiþ him ȝede,
Of godes help þat hadde nede,   392

þei wenten a non to here masse,
For here sinnen sscholde be þe lasse.

go to hear mass.

40 ¶ þo þe masse was iseid,   [337]
& þe uestement doun ileid,   396
þe king & roulond ifere,
Wente forþ as ȝe moun here,
Riȝt to þe paleis ȝate,
& founde houinge þer ate   400
Otuel, armed and idiȝt,
Al redi to bide fiȝt.
þo seide þat sarazin ;
" Sire king, where is þi cosin,   404
Roulond þat his truþe pliȝte,   [341]
þat he wolde wiþ me fiȝte ?
He was þo fol heie of mod,
Is he nou ilete blod."   408

After mass they all go out to the palace gate,

where they find Otuel ready and waiting for them.

He asks where Roland is.

41 ¶ Roulond stod & al[1] herde,
Hou otuel toward him ferde,
& answerde a non riȝt :
" By ihū, þat is fol of miȝt,   412
þin heued sschal fele vnder þin hood,
þat i nam nouȝt laten blood."

[1 MS. al &]

Roland declares he will soon show him what he can do.

42 ¶ " Wel-come be þou," quaþ otuwel þo,
& turnde his stede & made him go,   416
& to þe place þo rod he,
þere þe bataille sscholde be.
Al a-boute þe water ran,
þer was noþer man ne wimman,   420
þat miȝte in riden no gon,
At no stede bote at on ;
& þere otuwel in rood,
No lengere he ne a-bood.   424

They all ride to the place chosen for the fight;

it is a field surrounded by water except in one place, at which Otuel rides in first,

[fol. 270, back, col. 1.]

43 ¶ Roulond þat douȝti kniȝt,
Was fol hasteliche idiȝt,

but Roland is in such a hurry

& his stede he bi-strod,
& no lengere he ne abood,   428
Er þe dai i-don it were,
þer þei sschollen fiȝten ifere.
Anon als roulond be-heeld,
when he sees Otuel waiting for him,
Otuwel houede in þe feel[d],   432
Roulond was so egre to fiȝte,
þat for al þe world he ne miȝte
Abide to riden in at þe ȝate,
þere otuwel rod in ate,   436
He þoute þe nekste weie to ride,
& no lengere he nolde a-bide,
He smot his stede wiþ spores briȝte,
& wiþ help of godes miȝte,   440
that he makes his horse swim across the river.
Ouer þe water þe stede swam,
& to londe saf he cam.

44   ¶ Anon riȝt als roulond
Hadde ikauȝt þe druþe lond,   444
Gret enuye was ham be-twene,   [451]
At once they charge,
þei riden to-gedire wiþ speres kene,
þat were steue & nouȝt longe ;
& þe kniȝtes were boþ stronge,   448
& smyten eiþer in oþeres sscheld,
their horses fall, but they themselves are not hurt.
þat boþe hors fellen in þe feld,
& risen aȝein op *fram* þe grounde,
& boþe kniȝtes were hole & sounde.   452

45   ¶ þo þe stedes were risen boþe,
þe kniȝtes woxen boþ fol wroþe,
They draw their swords.
& drowen swerdes ate laste,
& eiþer huȝ on oþer faste.   456
Roland aims a stroke at Otuel,
Roulond to otuwel smot
A strok, þat fol sore bot,
He wolde haue smiten otuwel,
who dodges it,
& he blenkt swiþe wel,   460
& roulond smot þe stede broun,   [466]

& clef þe heued al adoun,
& þe stede fel to grounde,
Bot otuwel was hol & sounde.   464

and the sword cleaves the head of his horse.

46 ¶ Roulond was hende & good of wille,
& houede oppon his stede stille,
To smiten made he semblant non,
Er otuwel was risen & gon.   468

Roland waits for Otuel to get up.

[fol. 270, back, col. 2.]

47 ¶ " Roulond," quaþ otuwel, " what was þe?
Art tou blynd, miȝtou nouȝt se
Wil ich oppon mi stede sat?
Whi sscholde mi stede habbe that?   472
It hadde be more honour to þe,
For soþe to habbe i-smite me."

Otuel abuses him for killing his horse.

48 ¶ " Ouȝ," quaþ roulond, " blame me nouȝt,
Bisengeme, ihc habbe i-fouȝt.   476
Otuwel, ich hadde yment,
þat þou sscholdest haue ifeled þat dent.
Ich hadde wel leuere, so mote ich þe,
Otuwel, habbe ȝouen it þe."   480

"By Saint James," says Roland, "I meant the stroke for you."

49 ¶ Otuwel was wroþ his stede was slawe,
& wiþ his swerd he bar i-draue,
He smot to roulond wiþ good wille,
þat [h]ouede oppon his stede stille.   484
þat he hadde roulond ment,
& he failede of his dent,
& smot roulondes gode stede,
þat neuere eft on erþe he ne ȝede.   [478] 488

Otuel in a rage smites at Roland,

but misses him,

and kills his horse instead.

50 ¶ Otuwel þoute on errore deede,
þo he hadde slawe his stede,
Hou roulond houede stille as ston,
Til he was risen & gon ;   492
& he stod al stille,
& leet roulond risen at wille,
& seide, " roulond, so mote ich þe,
þat strok ich mente to þe,   496

Otuel gives Roland time to get up,

and declares he meant the stroke for him,

not for his horse.

& nou it is on þi stede istunt,
Let nou stonde du*n*t for dunt."

They fight fiercely
on foot.

51   ¶ Þo þei sien non oþer bote,
      þei wenten to-gidere al on fote,   500
      & strokes ȝeden bi-twene ham so kene,
      þat þe fer sprong out bi-twene.

52   ¶ King charles wiþ hise kniȝtes bolde, [486]
      Was come þe bataille to bi-holde,   504

Charles prays to
God, to
save Roland.

      & bi-souȝte god fol of miȝt,
      He sscholde saue roulond his kniȝt.

Roland, finding
that Otuel is a
strong knight,

53   ¶ Boþe kniȝtes were gode & stronge,
      & fouȝten to gider swiþe longe,   508
      Roulond was a hende kniȝt,

and smites hard,

      & feled þat otuwel smot ariȝt,

[fol. 271, col. 1.]

      & þat myȝt was in his arm,
      & þoute to sauen him *fra*m harm,   512
      & seide, " otuwel, let þi fiȝt,
      & leue on ihu ful of miȝt,

offers him
Belecent, the
king's daughter,
in marriage,
if he will
become Christian.

      & ich wele ben at acent,
      þat þou sschalt wedde belecent,   [521] 516
      þe kinges douȝter, mi nese þat is ;
      I rede, otuwel, þat þou do þis."

54   ¶ Quaþ otuwel to roulond,
      " Whil mi swerd is in min hond,   520
      Al þi preching is for nouȝt,

Otuel declares
nothing will make
him renounce his
religion.

      Hit ne cam neuere i*n* my þout,
      Me ne stant nouȝt of þe swich awe,
      þat þou sschalt make me reneie mi lawe,   524
      For to wedde belecent ;
      So nis nouȝt mi wille iwent."

55   ¶ Þo þei ne miȝte nouȝt acente,

The fight is
renewed.

      Aȝein to bataille þei wente,   528
      & fouȝten harde to-gidere beie ;
      Neueron of oþer ne stod eie.

56 ¶ Roulond bi-gan to meuen his blood,
þat otuwel so longe stood, 532
& for tene vp wiþ þe brond,
þat he bar in his hond,
& in þe heued he þoute to redde
Otuwel, bote nouȝt he ne spedde. 536
Otuwel starte o side,
& lette þe swerd bi him glide,
& roulond wiþ þe swerdes end,
Reiȝte Otuwel oppon þe lende ; 540
Als he wolde þe dent fle, [552]
Otuwel fel on kne.

57 ¶ Otuwel a-sschamed was,
þat he knelede oppon þe gras, 544
& for anger his herte gan sswelle,
& þouȝte roulonde for to quelle;
In the heued he hadde him ment,
Bote roulond bleinte for þe dent, 548
As swete ihu crist wolde,
þat roulond þere deie ne sscholde.
Bi side þe heued þe dent wente,
& þe hauberk he to-rente, 552
Fram þe hepe bon an heiȝ,
þat alle þe pece out fleiȝ.

58 ¶ King charles sauȝ þere he stood,
& was fol dreri in his mood, [574] 556
& was swiþe sore afriȝt,
To lese roulond his gode kniȝt,
For otuwel smot so heterliche,
þe king wende sikerliche, 560
þat roulond sscholde been ylore,
& was a sori man þere fore.

59 ¶ As þe king stod in doute,
He spak to his folk aboute, 564
& seide to alle þat þere were ;

<table>
<tr><td>and he bids all his knights to kneel and pray for an end of the duel, and</td><td></td><td>" Lordinges, doth as ich ȝou lere,
Sitte eche man oppon his kne,
& biddeth to god in trinite,
For his grace & for hise miȝtes,
Sende seiȝtnesse bi-twene þo kniȝtes</td><td>568</td></tr>
<tr><td>the conversion of Otuel.</td><td></td><td>& ȝiue otuwel wille to day,
For to reneien his lay."</td><td>572</td></tr>
<tr><td>They do so,</td><td>60</td><td>¶ Euerichone þei token here red,
& deden as þe king ham bed,
To ih'u crist þei deden here bone,
& swete ih'u herde ham sone.</td><td>[578] 576</td></tr>
<tr><td>and immediately a white dove descends from heaven and settles on Otuel's head.</td><td></td><td>A whit coluere þer cam fle,
þat al þe peple miȝten se,
On otuweles heued he liȝte,
þoru þe uertu of godes miȝte.</td><td>580</td></tr>
<tr><td>Otuel at once leaves off fighting,</td><td></td><td>& otuwel, þat douȝti kniȝt,
Wiþ-drouȝ him anoon riȝt
Fram roulond, & stod al stille,
To fiȝte more he ne hadde wille,
& séide, " Roulond þou smitest fol sore,
Wiþ-drau þin hond & smiȝt na more.</td><td>584
[582]</td></tr>
<tr><td>and says he will accept Roland's offer,</td><td></td><td>Ȝef þou wolt holden þat þou me het,
þat i sschal wedde þat maiden swet,
þe kinges douȝter, belesent,
For soþe, þan is mi wille went,
Ȝef i sschal wedden þat faire may,</td><td>588</td></tr>
<tr><td>and will become a Christian.</td><td></td><td>Ich wille bileuen oppon þi lay,
& alle myne godes forsake,
& to ȝoure god ich wille take."</td><td>592
[585]</td></tr>
<tr><td>Roland gladly agrees.</td><td>61</td><td>¶ Roulond likete þat word fol wel,
& answerede otuwel;
" I þonke it ih'u, ful of miȝt,
þorou wham þat grace is in þe liȝt."</td><td>596</td></tr>
<tr><td>[fol. 271, back, col. 1.]</td><td>62</td><td>¶ Otuel caste of his hond
Corsouse, his gode brond,</td><td>600</td></tr>
</table>

& roulond his also,
& to-gidere þei gune go.
Eyther for-ȝaf oþer his loþ,
Nas non of hem wiþ oþer wroþ,   604
Bote clippe & kusse eyþer oþer,   [588]
As eiþer hedde been oþeres broþer.

They both throw down their swords, and embrace each other, and walk off together.

63 ¶ King charles rood þidere a non,
   & kniȝtes wiþ him many on.   608
   Anon as he þider cam,
   Bi þe hon[d] roulond he nam,
   & seide, "roulond, for godes Erþe,
   Hou is þe and þis man iwurþe?   612
   So harde strokes as ȝe habben ȝiue,
   Hit is wunder þat ȝe liue."

Charles with his knights ride to meet them,

and asks what has happened.

64 ¶ "Sire," quaþ roulond, "we beþ al sounde,
   Noþer of vs ne haueth wounde.   [598] 616
   Otuwel haueþ his conseil nome,
   þat he wile cristene by-come,
   & ich habbe granted bi ȝoure acent,
   þat he sschal wedde belecent."   620

Roland tells him that Otuel has agreed to become Christian, if he may marry Belicent.

65 ¶ "Certes," quaþ charles þo,
   "Nou þou wolt þat it be so,
   I grante wel þat it so be,
   For whi þat he wille dwelle wiþ me.   624
   þanne hadde ich þe & oliuer,
   Otuwel, & gode ogger,
   In all þe world in lenkþe & brede,
   þer nis king þat nolde me drede."   628

Charles agrees at once.

66 ¶ þe king took otuwel a non,
   & to his paleis made him gon,
   & makeden murþe & meloudie,
   Of alle maner of menestrausie,   632
   For þe miracle þat was wrouȝt,
   þat otuwel hadde iturnd his þouȝt.

They all return to the palace,

and make great rejoicing for the conversion of Otuel.

67 ¶ On moruen þo þe day was briȝt,
þei ladden to churche þat noble kniȝt, 636
Bisschop turpin was bisschop þo,
He follede him þat day & nammo.

68 ¶ þo otuwel hadde follauȝt nome, [613]
& to þe kingges pees was come, 640
þe king beed him his douȝter a non,
& feire londes mani on.

69 ¶ Otuwel to þe king saide,
" Sire, keep me wel þat maide, 644
For soþe ich nele hire neuere wedde,
No neuere wiþ hire go to bedde,
Er þi werre to þe ende be brouȝt,
& sum what of þi wille wrouȝt, 648

Whan king garsie is slawe or take,
þanne is time mariage to make." [660]

70 ¶ Quaþ king charles to otuwel ;

" Nou i se þou louest me wel, 652
& ȝef i leue, so mote I þe,
þou ne sschalt nouȝt lese þi loue on me."

71 ¶ þo leet þe king asemblen a non,
Alle hise duzze peres echon. 656
"Lordinges," he seide, "what is ȝoure red, [663]
King garsie seiþ, i sschal be ded,
& as ȝe habbeþ iherd segge,
He þenkeþ cristendam to legge, 660

Wheþer wole we wenden oppon him anon,
Oþer abide til winter be gon ?"
þe duzze peres acentenden þer to,

To bide til winter were i-do, 664
& alle winter þe king of Fraunce,
Lette maken his purueianse.
Al þat winter at hom he bod, [685]
& in somer to werre he rod. 668

L Ordinges, boþe ȝinge & olde,
   Her[k]neþ as we formest tolde,
Hou þe werre was fol hyȝe,
Bitwene king charles & king garsie.   672
Anon as winter was ygon,
þe king a semblede his host a non,
& mochel peple cam to his hond   [697]
Out of mani diuerse lond.   676
Aueril was comen an winter gon,   [721]
& charles tok þe weie a non,
& drouȝ him to ward lumbardie,
To werren oppon king garsie.   680
þere was set wiþ outen faille
Certein day of bataille.

72   ¶ Anoon as charles was icome,
Niȝ honde þar þe bataille was nome,   684
In a mede a non riȝt
þe kinges pauilons were ipiȝt,
Vnder an hul besides a riuere,
& bi-fel as ȝe moun here.   688
Fol niȝ þe water þe king lay,
Of bataille for to a-bide his day,
& vppon þat oþer side,
He miȝte seen hise enemis ride,   692
& þere nas brugge ne forde non,
þat man miȝte ouer riden ne gon.

73   ¶ King charles þat gode kniȝt,
Tok carpenters a non riȝt,   696
& lette make a brugge a non,
þat men miȝten ouer gon,   [755]

74   ¶ þo þe brugge was al ȝare,
þat men miȝten ouer fare.   700
Hit bitidde vppon a day,
Wil charles in his bed lay,

Now I will tell
you of the war
with Garsie.

In the following
April Charles sets
out on his
campaign towards
Lombardy.

The tents are
pitched under a
hill,
near a river,
[fol. 272, col. 1.]

over which was
neither bridge
nor ford.

Then Charles
causes a bridge to
be made.

One day early

Roland, Oliver, and Ogier cross the river in search of adventures.

þat roulond an[d] oliuer,
& þe gode kniȝt oger,   704
Ouer þe brugge þei wenten ifeere,
Auntres for to sen & here.   [763]
& þo þei ouer passed were,
Such auntres þei funden þere,   708
For al þe good vnder sonne,
þei nolde habben þe gamen bi-gonne.

The same day four kings of Garsie's army,

75   ¶ Of garsies oft foure heþene kinges,
Wenten for to[1] here tidinges,   712
For alle cas þat miȝte bitide,
Wel i-armed bataille to bide.
Here foure names ȝe moun wite,
As we finden in romaunse write,   716

Turabeles,

76   ¶ Turabeles hatte þe to king,
A stout sarazin, wiþ-outen lesing ;

Balsamun,

77   ¶ þat oþer balsamun het,
A werse man ȝede non on fet ;   720

Astaward, and

78   ¶ Astaward was þe þriddes name,
He louede werre & hatede game ;

Clarel,

79   ¶ þe ferþe king hiȝte Clarel,[2]
þat neuere ȝite ne dede wel.   724

were out riding, hoping to meet with some of the French knights,

As þei riden alle yfere,
þat on seide as ȝe moun here ;
"Mahoun leeue ous ȝit abide,   [793]
In to Fraunce þat we moun ride,   728

but especially with Roland.

& ich miȝte roulond mete,
Al wiþ wraþþe ich wolde him grete :

[fol. 272, col. 2.]

þat traitour he slouȝ mi broþer,
Ne gete ich neue[r] eft such a noþer."   732

80   ¶ Roulonde herde & oliuer,
& þe gode kniȝt ogger,
Hou þei speken hare wordes hiȝe,

---

[1] MS. te.   [2] MS. Clar, the rest of the word being erased.

& þratten roulond to die ;   736
& roulond was so ny3,
þat alle foure kinges he sy3.

81   ¶ " Felawes," quaþ rouland a non,
" Ich am war of oure fon,   740
þei beþ foure, And we bote þre,
Daþeit habbe þat hem fle ;
Nou we habben fonnden game,
Gawe to hem a godesname !"   744

82   ¶ Anon as clarel ham sy3,
He seide, " oure enemys beþ ny3,
Ich se bi here cuntenaunse,
þei beþ cristene men of fraunce.   748
Charles ost liþ here bi-side,
In pauilons bataille to bide,
& þese beþ of hise men, i-wis,
þerfore mi reed is þis,[1]   752
þat we hasteliche to ham ride,
& loke wheþer þei wole abide."

83   ¶ Wiþ þat word þe kinges a non,
Touchede here stedes & made hem gon,   756
& toward þe cristene kni3tes þei riden,
& þei dou3tiliche a-biden.

84   ¶ Astaward wiþ roulond mette,
Nou3t he ne spak, ne him ne grette, [811] 760
Bot smot him wiþ his spere anon,
þorou þe sscheld he made hit gon.
& roulondes spere, y-wis,
Was wel betere than was his,   764
To astawardes herte hit 3ede,
& caste him doun of his stede,
" Aris," quaþ roulond, " & tak þe bet,
At this time þou art i-let."   768

Roland sees them,

and points them out to his companions.

Clarel espies the French knights,

and proposes to attack them,
[1 MS. istis]

which they do.

Astaward engages Roland,

but is slain by him.

85   ¶ Curabeles no lengere ne a-bood,
       To god ogger a non he rod ;
       Ogger was a strong kniȝt,
       & rod to him wiþ gret miȝt,   772
       & bar a-don hors & pak,
       & þe sarazins nekke to-brak.

86   ¶ Balsamum & oliuer,   [823]
       Eyþer neiȝede oþer ner ;   776
       Þo balsamum bi-gan to ride,
       Oliuer nolde no lengere a-bide ;
       He pingde his stede wiþ spores kene,
       & smot a strok þat was sene,   780
       He ne miȝte þo no bette do,

       Bote gurde þe nekkebon otwo.

87   ¶ Þus roulond & oliuer,
       & þe gode kniȝt ogger,   784
       Slouwen þe heþene kinges þre,
       & ȝit nolde nouȝt clarel fle :

       To þe duk roulond he rood,
       & roulond his strok a-bod.   788
       For wraþþe hise felaus were islein,
       He rood to roulond wiþ gret mayn,
       & bar a spere greet & long ;
       & the sarazin was strong,   792
       & in the sadel sat faste,

       & roulond to grounde he kaste.   [834]
       Wiþ þe fal þe steede a noon,
       To-barst þat o sschanke bon,   796
       Roulond vppon his feet stood,
       & ne hadde nouȝt bote good.

88   ¶ Ogger sauȝ fol wel þo,
       Þat roulondes hors was a-go,   800

       Ogger þat was douȝti of dede,
       Smot doun clarel of his stede.
       Oliuer tok þe stede a non,   [840]

& to roulond he gan gon.
" Roulond, haue þis," quaþ oliuer,
" Þis þe sente good ogger,
& clarel he haueþ to grounde iþrowe,
For he brouȝte þe so lowe." 804

whose horse Oliver seizes and brings to Roland.

808

89 ¶ Rouland þat hadde his stede ilore,
þonkede hem boþe þer fore,
& wos þe gladdeste man vnder sonne,
þat he hadde an hors i-wonne. 812

Roland thanks them both.

90 ¶ Clarel vppon his feet stood,
& fauȝt as he were wood,
On none manner he nolde fle,
Bot fauȝt aȝein hem alle thre. 816

Clarel will not fly, but stands his ground against all three.

91 ¶ Þe þre kniȝtes were fol stronge,
He ne miȝte nouȝt dure aȝein ham longe,
& seide to hem alle þre,
" Lordinges, let me o liue be : 820
To ȝou it were lutel honour, [850]
To sle me þat nabbe no socour."
To fiȝte more he for-sook,
& roulond his swerd he tok ; 824
Roulond was hende & nouȝt forsok,
& of clarel his swerd he tok.

[fol. 272, back, col. 2.]
He soon surrenders,

and gives up his sword to Roland.

92 ¶ " King clarel," quaþ ogger,
" Worþ vp bi-hinden me her." 828
Þo was king clarel glad,
For to do þat ogger bad,
& was staleworþe & liȝt,
& lep vp[1] a non riȝt. 832
Þo wenten þei forþ wiþ-outen targing,
& þoute presente charles þe king,
Wiþ clarel þat þei hadden i-nome,
& hopeden to ben welcome. 836
& of here weie þei were let,
& swiþe harde þei were met : [858]

Ogier bids Clarel get up behind him :

he does so, and they start homewards,
[1] MS. vt

þei sien of garsies men a feerd,
Boþe wiþ spere & wiþ swerd,   840
Bitwen hem & þe pauiloun,
þere þei sscholden wenden a-doun,
þei ne miȝte skapen *in* neuere a side,
þoru out hem þei mosten ride.   844

93 ¶ " Felawes," quaþ ogger þo,
To roulond & oliuer bo,
" Ich wene er we hom come,
Clarel ous worþ bynome ;   848
Lordinges, what is nou ȝoure red,
Wole we smiten of his hed ? "

94 ¶ Quaþ roulond, " so mote ich þe,
At þat red nel ich nouȝt be."   852
' No ich noþer," quat oliuer,
" Bi þe louerd sein Richer,

On liue i rede we leten him go,
& ne do we him na*m*more wo.   856
Such cas may fallen *in* sum neede,
He mai quiten vs oure mede."

95 ¶ " Bi god," quaþ ogger, " þat is soþ,
& where he do, or he ne doþ,   860
Hit where sschame to ous, iwis,
To sslen a man þat ȝolden him is :

I rede we leten him gon his wey,   [867]
For we moten tenden to a noþer pley."   864

96 ¶ Alle þre þei were at on,

& leten clarel on liue gon.
Clarel nolde no lengere a-bide,
He ne askede non hors onne to ride,   868
Bote on fote dede him go,
& leuede he*m* þare in muchel wo.

97 ¶ " Nou, lordinges," quaþ ogger
To Roulond & to oliuer,   872

" Ich wole triste to my sswerd,
& fonde forto passe þis ferd.
Ich hope, þoru help of godes miȝt,
To se mi lord charles þis niȝt.   876
Ȝef ani sarazin wiþ eie,
Comeþ to lette me of mi weie,
Selp me god & þis day,
He sschal abugge, ȝef ich may."   880

Ogier declares he
means to fight his
way home.

98   ¶ " Nou," quaþ roulond, þat douȝti kniȝt,
" & ich wille helpe þe bi mi miȝt ;
I nele to day bi sein martin,
Ȝilde me to no sarazin."   884

Roland says the
same,

99   ¶ Quaþ oliuer, " so mote ich þe,
In mani peril ich habbe ibe,
& yef ich faille at þis nede,
God ne lete me neuere eft spede ;   888
I nele, ȝef god halt me sound,
To day ȝelde me to non hound."

and so does Oliver,

100   ¶ þei markeden hem alle þre,
To him þat þolede deþ on tre,   892
& no lengere þei ne abiden,
Anon in to þe ferde þei riden.   [889]

and they charge
into the Saracens.

101   ¶ A sarazin wiþ roulond mette,
& of his weie roulond lette ;   896
He cam out of al þe here,
& bar to roulond a gret spere :
A bold kniȝt þat hatte byoun,
An[d] roulond bar him a-doun.   900

Byoun, a Saracen,
attacks Roland,

but is slain by
him.

102   ¶ Oliuer, þat was his broþer,
He mette wiþ a noþer,
A douȝti kniȝt, an heþene man,
A strong þef þat heet bassan.   904
Oliuer was horsed wel,
& bare a spere kene & fel,

Oliver charges
Bassan,

and rides him
down;

& smot him riȝt vnder þe sscheld,
þat þere he lay amidde þe feld.　　908

while Ogier cuts
down another
named Moter.

103　¶ & þe gode kniȝt ogger,
Mette wiþ on, þat heet moter,
& wolde him habbe doun i-bore,
& ogger was wroþ þar-fore,　　912
& smot þe sarazin so sore,
þat he ne spak neuere more.

Thus the French
knights exert
themselves,

104　¶ Oliuer, ogger, & Roulond,
Among þe sarazins stureden here hond,　　916
þoru help of god þat is a-boue,
þat ham hadde þat grace i-ȝoue.
þorou þe ferd as þei Riden,

and make great
slaughter
amongst the
Saracens.

Alle þat here strokes a-biden,　　920
þei were maimed for euere more.
þe douȝti kniȝtes þei smiten so sore,
þat wiþ-inne a litel stounde,
þei felden mani on to grounde.　　924

105　¶ þo cam a soudan, stout & firs,
On of garsies duzze peers,
þat hatte karmel of tabarie;　　[895]

Then Karmel of
Tabarie rallies his
men,

Oppon þe Sarasins he gan crie,　　928
" Recreiede kniȝtes, whi nele ȝe fiȝte,
Traitours, þeues, where [is] ȝoure miȝte?
It is sschame bi god mahon,
þat oure folk goon þus a doun."　　932

106　¶ Wiþ þis word, carmel a non
Pingde his stede & made him gon,

and charges at
Ogier,

& rood to ogger in þat hete,
& þoute he sscholde his lif for-lete;　　936
& was strong, & ful of tene,
& smot sore, & þat was sene.

whom he wounds
and unhorses,

He smot ogger in þe sscheld,
þat ogger lay amidde þe feld,　　940

Sore he fel oppon þe grounde,
& hadde a fol luþer wonde.

107   ¶ þe duk roulond þat sey3,
For wraþþe he was wod wel ny3,   944
& for wraþþe smot him so sore,   but is himself cut
þat he ne spak neuere eft more.   down by Roland.

108   ¶ þo cam anwe of nubie,   Then Anwe of
On of kinges kni3tes garsie,   948 Nabia unhorses
& felde oliuer to grounde,   Oliver,
Bote he ne 3af him neuere a wounde.

109   ¶ Roulond was fol wroþ wiþ alle,   [fol. 273, back,
þo he sau3 oliuer falle,   952   col. 1.]
& anawe of nubie he smot,   and he, too, is
þat neuere eft crouste he ne bot.   slain by Roland.

110   ¶ Oliuer ros ap fram þe grounde,   Oliver is soon up
Al hol wiþ-outen wonde,   again.
& a non his stede he nam,   956
& to roulond sone he cam.

111   ¶ þo was roulond fol fawe,
þat oliuer was nou3t isslauwe,   960
þo þei were to-gidere imet.   They two fight
þo were þei harde biset,   hard,
Amang sarasins þat were kene,
& þei smiten sore for tene.   964

112   ¶ Whil roulond fau3t & oliuer,
Heuere stode þe gode ogger,
& hadde lorn his gode stede,   but Ogier cannot
& his wounde gan faste blede ;   help them much
& 3it he fau3t þere he stod,   968 for his wound.
& leide on as he were wod.

113   ¶ Whil ogger, þat dou3ti kni3t,
A3enes sarazins stod in fi3t,   972
Oppon a stede Clarel come driue,   Clarel comes up,
þat ogger halp to sauen o liue,

þorou cunseil of roulond & oliuer.
& a non he knuȝ ogger, 976
"Ogger," he seide, "hit is my red,
Ȝilte to me[1] or þou art ded; [952]
þou holpe to saue mi lif a day,
Ich wole sauen þin, ȝef I may." 980

114 ¶ Ogger sauȝ wel wiþ his Eye
þat he was in point to deye,
& to clarel he gan gon,
& tok him his swerd a non. 984

115 ¶ Clarel nas no wedded man,
Clarel hadde a fair lemman,
þat was hoten aufanye,
& was born in Ermenie. 988

116 ¶ Clarel, anon riȝtes,
Clepede to him two kniȝtes,
& seide to hem anon;
"To mi lemman ȝe schulle gon, [956] 992
& segge þat ich sente hire þis kniȝt,
& þat his wounde be heled ariȝt;
& god hede to him nome,
To sauen him til mi to-come." 996

117 ¶ þe kniȝtes deden as he hem bad,
To his lemman he was lad,
þat was hoten aufanye, [962]
þat was kinges douȝter garsie, 1000
& ȝo was glad of þat present,
To do clareles comaundement.
Roulond & oliuer fouȝten,
þat of here liues nouȝt ne rouȝten. 1004
þei hadden fouȝten ouer myȝte,
þei ne miȝte no lengere dure to fiȝte,
An[d] a non turnden here steeden,
& flowen for þei ne myȝten nouȝt speden. 1008

118   ¶ To otuwel it was told,
      þat roulond þat was bold,
      Oliuer & ogger bo,
      Were ouer þe water go.   1012

Meanwhile Otuel hears that Roland, Oliver, and Ogier had crossed the river.

119   ¶ Otuwel a non riȝtes,
      Leet armen him, & alle hise kniȝtes ; [1024]
      þo he was armed & wel i-diȝt,
      He wente to þe king a non riȝt,   1016
      & seide, "sire, i dwelle to longe,
      Roulond, oliuer, an ogger þe stronge,
      Oue[r] þe water alle þre,
      Beþ went for envie of me,   1020
      To loke wher þei miȝten spede,
      To don any douȝti deede,
      Among þe sarazins bolde :
      & i sscholde be couward hoolde,   1024
      þer fore i nele no lengere abide ;
      To sechen hem ich wole ride.
      þauȝ þei habben envie to me,
      Ich wille for þe loue of þe,   1028
      Fonden whoþer i miȝte comen,
      [1]To helpen hem ar þei weren inomen.
      & ȝif hem any harm bytit,
      Let ham witen hare oune wit."   1032

He arms himself and his men,

goes to Charles,

and declares his intention of going to find and help them.

[1 MS. Te]

120   ¶ Quaþ þe king, "par charite,
      Otuwel, ich biseche þe,
      For godes loue hiȝe þe bliue,
      & fonde to sauen hem o liue,   1036
      Er þei be slawe or nome,
      & þe sschal sone socour come."

Charles begs to lose no time, but go at once.

121   ¶ Otuwel no lengere ne abood,
      Anon his stede he bi-strood,   1040
      & alle hise kniȝtes bi his side,
      & toward þe ferd he gan to ride.   [1029]

[fol. 274, col. 1.]

Otuel and his men at once start toward the ford,

122   ¶ A no*n* as otuwel was goon,
    þe king leet diȝte his host a non,   1044
    After otuwel to wende,
    As a god king & hende.

123   ¶ As otuwel bi-gan to ride,
    He lokede a-bouten i*n* eche side,   1048

    & he sauȝ ate laste,
    Where Roulond fleyȝ, & oliuer faste.
    Otuwel touchede his stedes side,   [1039]

    & aȝein hem he gan ride,   1052
    & seide, " turneþ aȝein a non,
    & helpeþ to wreke ȝou on ȝoure fon ;
    þei sschulle abugge, so mote ich þe,
    þat makeþ ȝou so faste fle."   1056

124   ¶ Þo þei herden otuwel speken,
    þat þei sscholden ben a-wreken,
    þo were þei ferchs to fiȝte,
    & tournden aȝein & were fol liȝte.   1060

125   ¶ " Lordinges," quaþ otuwel þo,
    " Whuder is god ogger go ? "
    & þei answereden, sikinge sore,

    " For soþe, we ne sien him nouȝt ȝore,   1064
    We ne witen where he is by-come,
    Wheþer he is islawe oþer nome."

126   ¶ " Allas ! allas ! " quaþ otuwel,
    " þis tiding likeþ me nout wel ;   1068
    Sire charles, my lord þe king,
    Wole be sori for þis tiding.

    For godes loue, hie we bliue,
    & loke we whoþer ogger be a liue."   1072

O tuwel & oliuer,
    & Roulond þat douȝti bacheler,
    Wiþ a feir compaignye,
    þei bigunnen for to hie,   1076

Toward king garsies host,
For to a-baten of hare bost.

127 ¶ þere was a sarazin strong,   A Saracen,
  þat bar a brod swerd & a long, 1080
  & was hoten encumbrer,   Encumbrer,
  & bigan to neiȝen hem ner,
  Oppon a muche blak stede ;   [fol. 274, col. 2.]
  & otuwel took of him hede, 1084
  & of his armes hadde a siȝt,
  & knuȝ him a non riȝt :
  & no lengere he ne abod,
  Otuwel to him rood,   1088 is borne down by
  & bar him doun hors & man, [1055] Otuel,
  þus otuwel gamen bi-gan.

128 ¶ Estuȝt of legers, a noble kniȝt, while Estught
  þat wiþ otuwel cam to fiȝt, 1092 slays another,
  Bar a spere of tre, fol fin,
  & smot a bold sarazin,
  In to þe bodi þoru þe sscheld,
  & þere he lay det in þe feld. 1096
  Oliuer ho slouȝ a noþer,   and Oliver and
  & þe ferþe roulond his broþer. Roland two
            more.

129 ¶ þo þe freinche kniȝtes seien,
  þe sarasins fallen wiþ hare eien, 1100
  þei nolden þo no lengere abide, Soon they make
  þei smiten to in Eche side, the Saracens fly.
  & felden sarazins faste,
  & þei flowen ate laste. 1104

130 ¶ King clarel made hem torne aȝein, Clarel rallies
  Oppon cristene men to lein, [1124] them,
  & he leide on faste,
  & þe þef ate laste,   1108
  Slou dromer of alemaine ; and slays Dromer.
  þat rue fol sore þe king charlemaine

<table>
<tr><td>Erpater, king of
India,</td><td>131</td><td>¶ Erpater king of ynde was,</td><td></td></tr>
<tr><td></td><td></td><td>He cam wiþ a mase of bras,</td><td>1112</td></tr>
<tr><td>smites Otuel;</td><td></td><td>& otuwel on þe helm he reiʒte,</td><td></td></tr>
<tr><td></td><td></td><td>So harde þat al þe heued to-queiʒte.</td><td></td></tr>
<tr><td></td><td>132</td><td>¶ Quaþ otuwel, " so mote y þe,</td><td></td></tr>
<tr><td></td><td></td><td>Ich ne þoute nauʒt boruwe þat strok of þe ; 1116</td><td></td></tr>
<tr><td></td><td></td><td>Bi min heued vnder myn hat,</td><td></td></tr>
<tr><td></td><td></td><td>I nele nouʒt longe ouwe þe þat.'</td><td></td></tr>
<tr><td>but Otuel cleaves
him in two.</td><td></td><td>Otuwel, wiþ a fauchoun,</td><td></td></tr>
<tr><td></td><td></td><td>Cleef him al þe heued a-doun,</td><td>1120</td></tr>
<tr><td></td><td></td><td>& he fil vnder his horse feet.</td><td></td></tr>
<tr><td></td><td></td><td>Quaþ otuwel, " þat Ich þe bi-heet."</td><td></td></tr>
<tr><td>The French press
on,</td><td>133</td><td>¶ Þo was otuwel fol of mood,</td><td></td></tr>
<tr><td></td><td></td><td>& fauʒt as he were wood.</td><td>1124</td></tr>
<tr><td></td><td></td><td>Al þe kinges ost a non,</td><td></td></tr>
<tr><td></td><td></td><td>Foleuweden otuwel Echon,</td><td></td></tr>
<tr><td>[fol. 274, back,
col. 1.]</td><td></td><td>Roulond & oliuer,</td><td></td></tr>
<tr><td></td><td></td><td>& maden a foul larder.</td><td>1128</td></tr>
<tr><td>and at last the
Saracens fly.</td><td></td><td>Þe kniʒtes leiden on so faste.</td><td></td></tr>
<tr><td></td><td></td><td>Þe sarazins flouwen ate laste.</td><td></td></tr>
<tr><td>Night comes on;</td><td>134</td><td>¶ Þo neiʒede it toward eue,</td><td></td></tr>
<tr><td></td><td></td><td>Þo moste þe ost bileue,   [1129] 1132</td><td></td></tr>
<tr><td>they leave off
fighting,</td><td></td><td>& dwellen þere al þat niʒt,</td><td></td></tr>
<tr><td></td><td></td><td>Til on morwe þe dai was briʒt.</td><td></td></tr>
<tr><td></td><td></td><td>Þo þe ost was wiþ drawe,</td><td></td></tr>
<tr><td></td><td></td><td>To resten hem, as is þe lawe,</td><td>1136</td></tr>
<tr><td>and in the morn-
ing Clarel comes
with a flag of
truce,</td><td></td><td>King clarel kam in fourme of pees,</td><td></td></tr>
<tr><td></td><td></td><td>Wiþ tweie felawes, mo ne lees,</td><td></td></tr>
<tr><td></td><td></td><td>Toward charles ost, þe king,</td><td></td></tr>
<tr><td></td><td></td><td>For to wyten a tiding :</td><td>1140</td></tr>
<tr><td></td><td></td><td>& otuwel aʒein him wente,</td><td></td></tr>
<tr><td></td><td></td><td>To wite who him þidere sente.</td><td></td></tr>
<tr><td></td><td>135</td><td>¶ Þanne seide king clarel,</td><td></td></tr>
<tr><td></td><td></td><td>To þe douʒti otuwel,   [1136] 1144</td><td></td></tr>
</table>

"Kniȝt," he seide, "so mote þou þe,
Tel me what þi name be,
þou art so douȝti man of dede,
& mani a kniȝt hauest maked blede,   1148
Ich wolde fol fain bi myn Eye,
Bringe þi name to þe king garsie."

and asks Otuel his name.

136   ¶ "Bi god, felawe," quaþ otuwel,
"Er þis þou kneuwe my name fol wel,   1152
So god sschilde me fram sschame,
Otuel is my cristine name :
Mahun ich habbe for sake,
& to ih'u ich habbe me take."   [1143] 1156

Otuel tells him, and how he is now a Christian.

137   ¶ "Allas !" quaþ clarel, "whi destou so?
So wrecheliche hauestou do.
ȝit i rede[1] þou turne þi mood,
& leef on mahoun, ore þou art wod,   1160
& ich wole pese, ȝef þou wilt,
þat þou hauest garsie a-gult."
"Fiȝ," quaþ otuel þo,
"On mahoun & on garsie bo.   1164
Bi him þat maude adam & eue,
Y nele neuere oppon ȝou leue.
Bi ih'u, þat is fol of miȝt,
& ich may mete him ariȝt,   1168
þere sschal no sarazin skape oliue,
þat ich may hente, so mote ich þriue."

Clarel begs him to recant,

[1 MS. rere]

but Otuel scorns

and threatens him.

138   ¶ "Otuwel," quaþ clarel þo,
"Were we sumware, bitwene vs two,   1172
Bi mahoun, þat ich onne bileue,
Oppon þi bodi ich wolde preue,
þat mahoun may mo miracles make,
þan he þat þou art to itake :   1176
He nis nouȝt half, be mi croun,
So miȝty, as is sire mahoun."

[fol. 274, back, col. 2.]
Clarel challenges him to single combat,

<table>
<tr><td>which Otuel
readily accepts.</td><td>139</td><td>¶ Quaþ otuwel, "bi godes miȝte,</td><td></td></tr>
<tr><td></td><td></td><td>Clarel, mi truþe ich þe pliȝte,</td><td>1180</td></tr>
<tr><td></td><td></td><td>Whan euere þou wolt, hit schal be,</td><td></td></tr>
<tr><td></td><td></td><td>Euele mote he þriue þat fle."</td><td></td></tr>
</table>

Clarel proposes to fight the next morning,

if he can trust to have fair play.

140   ¶ Quaþ clarel, a non riȝt :

"Bi mahoun, þat is fol of miȝt,   1184

Woltou sikere me on hond,

þat no man of king charles lond,

Schal do me no vileynie,

By þe deaþ þat isschal deye,   1188

Mi conseil is a non inome,

To morue erliche ich wille come."

Otuel promises none shall touch him save himself,

141   ¶ Quaþ otuwel, " ne doute þe nouȝt.

Bi god, þat al þe world haueþ wrouȝt,   1192

& þe deþ þat ischal deie,

þou ne sschalt hente no vileinie,

Of no man of king charles lond,

Bote riȝt of myn oune hond :   1196

Bi him, þat made leef & bouȝ,

þer offe þe sschall þinken ynouȝ."

on which Clarel agrees.

Quaþ clarel, " þo do þi best,

To-morwe þou sschalt finde me prest."   1200

142   ¶ þus þe were þere boþe at on,   [1164]

Er þei wolden o twinne gon.

Eyþer oþer his treweþe pliȝte

Oppon Morwen for to fiȝte.   1204

Early next morning Clarel comes to the fight ready armed.

143   ¶ On moruwen þo þe day sprong,

Clarel þe king þouȝte long

To þe pauiloun til he cam,

To holde þe day, þat he nam :   1208

Oppon a stede wel idiȝt

He cam fol redi to bide fiȝt.   [1212]

Charles and his knights come out to see him.

144   ¶ King charles wiþ hise kniȝtes bolde,

Comen out clarel to bi-holde,   1212

Hou he com al redi diȝt,
Boldeliche to bide fiȝt.

145   ¶ Clarel was bold on his bond,
For [O]tuwel sikerede him on hond,   1216
þat no man of flechs & blood,
Ne sscholde doon him nouȝt bote good,
Bot hem selue tweien fiȝte,
& habbe þe maistrie who so miȝte.   1220
þo was clarel fol trist,
For to segge what him lust.

Clarel, relying on
Otuel's word,
has no fear,

146   ¶ King charles was an old man,
& clarel hede þer offe nam,   1224
& seide, "charles, þou art old,
Who made þe nou so bold,
To werren oppon king garsie,
þat is cheef of al painie?   1228
Al paynime he haued in wold,
þou dotest, for þou art so hold."   [1252]

and mocks at
Charles for daring
at his age to war
on Garsie,
the chief of all
heathendom.

147   ¶ King charles waryþede anon riȝt,
þat clarel tolde of him so liȝt,   1232
& hadde iment þo fol wel,
To habben ifouȝten wiþ clarel :
& bad fetten his armure briȝt,
& wolde armeu him a non riȝt;   1236
& seide in wraþþe, "by godes miȝte,
Ich mi self wole wiþ him fiȝte."

Charles is
enraged,

and wants to fight
him himself;

148   ¶ Roulond bi þe king stood,
& bi-gan to meuen his mood,   1240
& sede to þe king a non,
"þou hauest, sire king, mani on,
Gode douȝti kniȝtes of deede,
To fiȝte þi self þou ne hauest no nede."   1244

but Roland says
there are plenty of
others ready to
fight for him.

149   ¶ "God sschilde, sire," quaþ oliuer,
"Hit sscholde springe fer or ner,

Oliver also
protests;

[fol. 275, col. 1.]

To putte þin oune bodi to fiȝt,
& hauest so mani a douȝti kniȝt." 1248

150 ¶ King charles swor his oþ,
& bi-gan to wexe wroþ,
& seide, "for ouȝt þat man may speke,
Miself, ich wile ben on him wreke." [1260] 1252

151 ¶ "A! sire," quaþ otuwel þo,
" For godes loue sei nouȝt so,
Ich & he beþ truþe pliȝte,
þat we sschole to-gidere fiȝte,   [1263] 1256
& ich wole telle þe, wiþ oute faille,
Where fore we habbe taken bataille.

152 ¶ He wolde habbe maked me ȝusterday,
To habbe reneied my lay,   1260
& seide, þat ich was ilore

& god nas nouȝt of marie bore :
& seide, algate he wolde preue,
þat ich am in mis beleue.   1264
þere-fore he profreþ him to fiȝt,
To wite wheþer is more of miȝt,
Ih'u, þat is louerd min,
Or mahoun & apolyn.   1268
þous we habbeþ þe bataille inome,
& boþe we beþ iswore to come."

153 ¶ Quaþ þe king charles þo,
" Otuwel, whan it is so,   1272
Tak þe bataille a godes name,
& ih'u schilde þe fram sschame !"

Otuwel, þat noble kniȝt,
Lette armen him a non riȝt,   1276
& his gode stede bistrod,
& no lengere he ne abood,

Bote to þe stede he rood fol riȝt,
þere clarel houede to bide fiȝt.   1280

154 ¶ Anon as otuwel was icome
Here conseil was a non inome,
No lengere þei ne abiden,
Anon riȝt togidere þei riden, 1284 The fight at once begins.
Noon oþer nas ham bitwene,
Bote gode stronge speres & kene.
Nas neuer noþer of oþer agast,
& eiþer sat in his sadel fast, 1288
þat boþe stedes ȝeden to grounde, They are both unhorsed,
& þe kniȝtes weren al sounde ; [1301]
& boþe stedes wenten forþ,
þat on souþ, þat oþer norþ ; 1292
þe kniȝte on fote to-gidere ȝede, and they continue the fight on foot.
An drowen hare swerdes gode at nede,
Ne sparede þei nouȝt þe swerdes egge ;
Eyþer on oþer bi-gan to legge. 1296

155 ¶ þei were boþe swiþe stronge,
& fouȝten to-gidere swiþe longe.
King clarel was wel neȝ wood, Clarel gets angry,
þat otuwel so longe stood : 1300
In gret wraþþe otuwel he smot, and stuns Otuel with a blow on the helmet.
& his swerd felliche bot,
& þau þe swerd [nere] neuere so good, [fol. 275, back, col. 1.]
þe gode helm it wiþ-stood. 1304
Bote otuwel astoneied was,
þere he stood vp on þe gras.

156 ¶ Quaþ otuwel, " so mote ich go,
He ne louede me nouȝt, þat smot me so, 1308
Ich warne þe wel, so mote ich þe, Otuel says he will return as good,
þou sschalt habbe as good of me."

157 ¶ Otuwel, for wraþþe, a non
Areiȝte him on þe cheke bon ; 1312 and bares Clarel's cheek,
Al þe fel of þat was þare,
& made his teþ al bare. [1320]

158   ¶ þo otuwel sauȝ is cheke bon,
He ȝaf clarel a skorn a non,   1316

& seide, " clarel, so mote þou þe,
Whi scheuwestou þe teþ to me,
I nam no toþ drawere,   [1323]
þou ne sest me no cheine bere."   1320

159   ¶ Clarel felede him wounded sore,
& was maimed for euere more,

An smot to otuwel wiþ al his miȝt ;
& otuwel, þat douȝti kniȝt,   1324
Wiþ his swerd kepte þe dent,
þat clarel him hadde iment,
& yit þe dent glood adoun,

& smot otuwel oppon þe croun.   1328

160   ¶ Quaþ otuwel, " bi godes ore,
Sarazin þou smitest fol sore,
Suþen þi berd was ischaue
þou art woxen a strong knaue."   1332

161   ¶ Otuwel smot clarel þo,
O strok & nammo,
þat neuer eft word he ne spak,
& so otuwel his tene wrak.   [1339] 1336

162   ¶ þo was charles glad ynouȝ,
þat otuwel king clarel slouȝ,

& ȝaf otuwel, þat douȝti kniȝt,
A god Erldam þat selue niȝt.   1340

Al þat in þe ost was,
Maden murþe & solas,
þat otuwel hadde so bigunne,
& hadde so þe maistri wonne ;   1344
Al þat miȝt ouer al þe ost,
þei maden al þer ioye most.

163   ¶ þer cam a messager & browȝte tiding,
To garsie þat riche king,   1348

þat otuwel, his cosin in lawe,
Hadde king clarel i-slawe.

164 ¶ þo garsie it vnder-ȝat,   [1345]
      He was swiþe sori for þat.   1352
      & for wraþþe þere he stood,
      Corsede hise godes, as he were wood,
      & seide, " allas & walawo !
      Nou is gode clarel go.   1356
      Certes myn herte it wile to-breke,
      Bote ich mowe clarel a-wreke."

165 ¶ þo lette garsie asemlen a non,
      Alle hise sarazins echon,   1360
      & þouȝte þoru out alle þing
      To ben a-wreken on charles king,
      & on his cosin otuwel ;
      & on him self þe wreche fel.   1364

166 ¶ King charles herde be a spye,
      þat garsie þratte him to die,
      & he a-semblede hise kniȝtes echon,
      & sede to hem alle a non,   1368
      " Lordinges, garsie þinkeþ to ride,
      For soþe i nele no lengere a bide."
      þe king armede him a non,
      & alle hise kniȝtes echon,   1372
      þe king gurde him wiþ his swerd,
      & wente him self wiþ his ferd.

167 ¶ þe king cam stilleliche wiþ his ost,
      & garsie cam wiþ gret bost,   1376
      þo þe ostes neiȝeden nieȝ,
      þat eiþer ost oþer sieȝ,
      Out of garsies ost cam ride,
      A turkein þat was ful of prude ;   1380

168 ¶ Roulond was good & hende,   [1381]
      & aȝenes him gan wende,

þe tourkein no lengere nabod,

and charges
Roland,

To roulond a non he rood, 1384

& gurde roulond wiþ a spere,

þat wel couþe a strok bere;

& as douȝti as he was,

who loses one
stirrup.

His o stirop he las. 1388

169 ¶ Roulond was a-schamed þarfore,

þat he hadde his stirop lore,

[fol. 276, col. 1.]
Roland with
Durindal cuts
him down.

& wiþ dorendal, þat was good,

He smot þe tourkein oppon þe hood, 1392

& he sey doun of his stede;

So rowlond quitte him his mede.

Quaþ roulond, "þat ich þe biheet,

þou nult na more stenden on þi feet; 1396

Min o stirop þou madest me tine,

Nou hauestou lose boþe þine." [1392]

Another Saracen, 170 ¶ þer cam a noþer stout sarazin,

þat was armed wel a fin, 1400

Myafle, þat hiȝte myafle of bagounde,

& wiþ a litel stounde

He made his stede swiþe to goon,

wounds Oliver. & smot oliuer a noon 1404

þorou out al his armure briȝt,

He woundede sore þat gode kniȝt.

171 ¶ Roulond sauȝ þe contenaunse, [1400]

[1 MS. le]

His broþer was hurt wiþ þe[1] launce; 1408

Roland comes to
his aid,

His wardecors a non he fond,

& tok a spere out of his hond,

& made his hors make a sturt,

To him þat hadde his broþer hurt; 1412

and kills Myafle. & touchede him wiþ þe speres ord,

þat neuere eft he ne spak word;

& tok myafles stede a non,

& sette oliuer þer on. 1416

172 ¶ þere was a noble sarazin,
A king þat heet galatyn,
& cam wiþ a compainie,
& bigan faste to hie.   1420
Otuwel was war of þat,
Oppon his stede þere he sat,
Hou king galatin cam wiþ wille,
Cristene men for to spille.   1424
Wiþ þe spores þe stede he nam,
To galatyn þe king he kam.
þorou þe bodi he him bar,
& bad he scholde eft be war   1428
Of such a strok, whan it kam.
Non oþer hede of him he ne nam,
Bote rood forþ oppon his stede,
& leet þe sarazin ligge & blede.   1432

Galatyn next rides out,

but is at once killed by Otuel.

173 ¶ þo smiten þo ostes to-gidere a non,
& fouȝten faste & good won :
& to-daschsten many a scheld,
Mani a bodi lay in þe feld.   1436

Then ensues a general engagement.

[fol. 276, col. 2.]

174 ¶ þo cam ouer þe doune ride,
An heþene king, fol of prude,
& browȝte wiþ him al ferche þo,
A þousende sarazins & mo,   1440
& fouȝten faste a good stounde,
& felden cristene men to grounde.

A reinforcement of 1000 Saracens come up;

175 ¶ A douȝti bacheler cam ride,
Oppon king charles side,   [1429] 1444
A ȝong kniȝt, þat sprong furst berd,[1]
Of no man he nas aferd ;
Fiue hundred men wiþ him he brouȝte,
þat of hare lif litel þei rouȝte :   1448
Nas non twenti winter old,
& echon was douȝti man & bold.

[1 MS. herd.]

but five hundred young French knights

He hadde ichosen hem fol wide,
Bolde men bataille to bide.   1452
þei fouȝten faste wiþ inne a stounde,
& brouȝten sarazins to grounde :
þei were bolde & fouȝten faste,
þe sarazins flouwen ate laste.   1456
Roulond & oliuer hulpen wel,
& þe douȝty otuwel.

176   ¶ Coursabex, þe king, cam þo,
& mette fleinde a þousend & mo,   1460
" Traitours," quaþ coursabex, þe king, [1450]
" Certes þis is a foul þing,
þat ȝe schule fle for ferd :
Traitours, tourneþ aȝein þe herd,[1]   1464
Tourneþ aȝein alle wiþ me,
& we wole make þe freinche fle."
þous coursabex him self allone,
Made tourne hem aȝein echone.   1468

177   ¶ þe ȝinge kniȝt þat was so bold,
Riȝt nou þat ich offe habbe told,
Wiþ coursabex wel sone he mette,
& wiþ his swerd a non he sette   1472
Such a strok oppon his croun,
þat of his stede he fel a doun.
þe ȝinge kniȝt to him cam,
& coursabex o liue nam,   1476
& sente him charles þe king.   [1489]
þo was he glad of þat tiding.

178   ¶ þo þe tourkeins seien alle,
þat coursabex was falle,   1480
& cristene men smite sore,
þei flouwen & nolde fiȝte na more.
& þe gode ȝinge kniȝt,
Suwede & leidon doun riȝt.   1484

soon put them to flight.

Coursabex meets them flying,

[1 MS. berd.]

and rallies them,

but a young French knight

unhorses Coursabex

and takes him prisoner.

[fol. 276, back, col. 1.]

Then all the Saracens again begin to fly.

þere ne halp nou3[t] sire mahoun,
þe tourkeins 3eden faste a-doun.

179 ¶ þo kam poidras of barbarin,
& wiþ him mani a sarazin. 1488
Poidras oppon the 3unge kni3t
Leid on wiþ al his mi3t,
& here men to-gidere huwen,
& heþene hornes faste blewen ; 1492
Poidras & þe 3inge kni3t,
Bitwene hem was strong fi3t,
Poidras hadde þe more mayn,
& hadde wel nei3 þe kni3t slain. 1496

180 ¶ Otuwel, þat dou3ti kni3t,
Was war of þat a non ri3t.
Otuwel no lengere nabood,
To poidras a noon he rood, 1500
& smot poidras of barbarin,
þat þere he lay as a stiked swin.

181 ¶ Otuwel rood in to þe feerd,
& leide on faste mid his swerd. 1504
Roulond & oliuer,
Ne[i]3eden¹ otuwel ner,
& þe berdles kni3t,
& slowen sarazins a-doun ri3t. 1508

182 ¶ King garsie herde wiþ inne a stounde,
Hou hise men 3eden to grounde :
King garsie hadde a conseiler,
& a non he took him neer, 1512
& seide to him, " sire arperaunt,
A3enes otuwel myn herte stant,
þat þous haueþ reneid his lay,
& sleþ mine men ni3t & day. 1516
Sire arperant, what is þi reed [1513]
þat þe þef traitour nere ded ?

Poidras attacks
Charles's young
knight,

and nearly slays
him,

but Otuel sticks
Poidras like a pig.

Otuel and the
beardless knight
make great havoc
among the
Saracens.

[¹ MS. Ne 3eden]

Garsie consults
Arperaunt how
they are to kill or
take Otuel.

Certes fraunce hadde be wonnen,
Ne hadde his tresoun be bigunnen."   1520

183   ¶ " King garsie," quaþ arperaunt,
"Bi mahoun þat ȝonder stant,
Al þe while þat roulond
Mai bere durendal in his hond,   1524
& oliuer rit by his side,
For no þing þat may betide,
þou ne schalt neuere otuwel winne,
For nouȝt þat euere þou kans biginne."   1528
þo was garsie wel nyȝ wood,
For wraþþe on molde þere he stood.

184   ¶ þere was an affrikan gent,
þat hatte baldolf of aquilent,   1532
King garsie seide to him anoon ;
" Certes, Baldoff, þou most goon,
& take wiþ þe kniȝt & swein,
& tourne þe cristene men aȝein ;   1536
& ich mi self wole after come,
& helpe þat otuwel were nome."

185   ¶ Quaþ baldolf, " bi sire mahun,
Louerd, we wole don what we moun,   1540
& com þou after & tak hede,
Wuche maner þat we spede,
& ȝef þou sest þat nede be,
Com & help us er we fle,   1544
For whan an ost to fliȝt is went,
Bote socour come, it is schent."

186   ¶ Baldolf took his compainie,
& to þe bataille he gan heye,   1548
& wiþ inne a litel stounde,
Hard bataille þei habben i-founde.

187   ¶ Otuwel, douȝti of dede,
Where þei comen he took hede,   1552

& no lengere he ne bood,
Bote hasteliche to ham he rood.
Roulond & oliuer,
Neiȝeden otuwel ner,   1556
& þe gode ȝinge kniȝt,
þat was so douȝti man in fiȝt.
þo þei foure weren ifere,
þo miȝte men seen & here   1560
Harde strokes dele & diȝte,
& wiþ sarazins boldeliche fiȝte.

188   ¶ þer cam out of garsies ost,
    A man þat made muche bost,   1564
    A king þat hatte karnifees,
    & muchel onour þere he les.

189   ¶ þer kam a kniȝt of agineis,
    A bold man, & a courteis,   1568
    & wiþ carnifees he mette,
    & wende Carnifees to lette :
    King karnifees him haueþ istunt,
    & slouȝ him ate forme dunt.   1572
    þo karnifees hadde þous do,
    He wende to seruen ham alle so ;

190   ¶ Otuwel no lengere na-bood,
    To karnifees a non he rood ;   1576
    Karnifees knuȝ otuwel,
    By hise armes swiþe wel,
    & seide to þe godę gome,
    " For-sworne þef, artou come ? "   1580
    " Bi mahoun," quaþ karnifees,
    " þou schalt hoppen heuedles."

191   ¶ Otuwel, wiþ oute targing,
    Answerede karnifees þe king,   1584
    " Bi sein geme, ich ne habbe nouȝt munt,
    þa þou schalt ȝiue me þat dunt."

Otuel rides out to meet him,

followed by Roland, Oliver,

and the young knight.

[fol. 277, col. 1.]

Karnifees slays a knight of Agineis.

Otuel rides forward to engage him.

Karnifees knows Otuel,

þei nolden no lengere abide,
Anon to-gidere þei gunde ride :   1588

and attacks him,

Karnifees smot otuwel,
Biside þe heued þe strok fel,

and cuts off part
of his shield,

A corner of otuweles scheld
He gurde out amidde þe feld.   1592

192 ¶ Quaþ otuwel, " good it wite,
þat strok was wel ismite.
Nou þou schalt, bi seint martyn,
Preuen a strok of myn."   1596

but Otuel with one
blow kills him.

Otuwel karnifees smot,
Wiþ Corsouse þat wel boot,
þat karnifees souȝte þe ground,
Ros he neuere eft, hol ne sound.   1600

193 ¶ Þo þe sarazins wisten alle,
þat karnifees was ifalle,
& þat he nolde na more arise,

The Saracens are
panic-stricken,

þo bigan ham alle to agrise :   1604
For in al garsies feerd,
Nas such a man to handle a swerd.

and flee,

þo tournde þei to fliȝt,
þe sarazins a non riȝt.   1608

[fol. 277, col. 2.] 194 ¶ Þous þe gode otuwel,
& roulond þat was good & snel,
þoru þe help of godes miȝt,
Maden þe sarazins tourne to fliȝt,   1612
þrou swete ih'u cristes grace,

pursued by Otuel
and Roland.

& þei suweden faste þe chasse.
þe sarazins were so a dredde,
In to þe water manye fledde,   1616

[1 MS. smūme.]
Many of them are
drowned.

Summe swumme[1] & summe sunke,
& coold water ynouȝ þei drunke,

195 Til Roulond & oliuer þe gode, [1543]

[2 MS. mananie.]

In manie[2] harde stoures stode.   1620

Godde ogger in p*ri*soun lay,
.Boþe bi niȝt, & eke be day,
Herkneþ, what hede good to him nam,
& hou he out of p*ri*soun kam. 1624

196 ¶ Seuene heþene kniȝtes bolde,
Ogger was bi-taken to holde,
& þe foure ogger slouȝ,
& ȝit he skapede wel inouȝ. 1628

197 ¶ þere was a noble skuier,
þat wiþ queintize halp ogger.
Swiþe p*ri*ueliche & stille
He brouȝte ogger, to his wille, 1632
His swerd & his armure briȝt,
& ogger armede him a non riȝt.
þo[1] he hadde on his gode wede,
þe squier brouȝte him a good stede. 1636
Ogger no lengere ne abood,
þe goodde stede he bistrood, [1551]
þe squier was armed, & wel idiȝt,
& hadde a good hors & a liȝt ; 1640
& also stille as a ston
þe squier lep to horse a non,
& to þe porteres windou he kam,
& in his hond his mase he nam, 1644
& oppon þe windou he schof,
þat þe windou al to-drof.

198 ¶ Hit was abouten mid niȝt,
& the porter was a-friȝt, 1648
& asked a non, who was þare,
& who makede al þat fare.

199 ¶ " Porter," quaþ þe squier þo,
' Vndo þe gate & let us go. 1652
We here tellen, bi sire mahoun,
þat cristene men goon alle a doun,

Meanwhile Ogger lies in prison,

guarded by seven knights,

of whom he slays four.

A squire brings him his arms,

[1 MS. þe]

and a horse.

They ride off secretly.

The squire breaks the porter's window.

The porter demands who is there.

[fol. 277, back, col. 1.]

I

& ich & mi felawes iwis,
We wole witen hou it is,　　　　　1656
& ȝef we ani good winne,
For soþe þou schalt parten þer inne."

& he dude op þe ȝate wide,
& lette ham boþe out ride,　　　　　1660
& steek aȝein þe gate fast,
& þere þei sien ogger last.

200　¶ Ogger rood al þat niȝt,
Til on þe morewen þe day was briȝt ;　　1664
þat neuere his feet comen on grounde,
Er he hadde his felawes founde.

201　¶ þo roulond & oliuer
Weren war of gode ogger,　　　　　1668
þei were fol glad of þat siȝt,　　[1558]
& þonkeden ih'u fol of miȝt.

202　¶ þo roulond & oliuer,
Adden imet wiþ gode [Ogger]　　　1672
þei were also fous to fiȝt,
As euere was a foul to fliȝt ;

& wenten in to þe bataille a non,
& fouȝten faste & good won,　　　　1676
& made þe sarazins a-gaste,
& otuwel nas nouȝt þe laste.

203　¶ þo alle foure weren ifere,
þar nere none strokes dere,　　　　1680
þo douȝti kniȝtes smiten so sore,
As þauȝ þei ne hadden nouȝt fouȝten ȝore,

þat wiþ inne a litel stounde,
Sarazins ȝeden alle to grounde.　　　1684

204　¶ King garsie toke god hede,
Hou his folk to grounde ȝede,

& no lengere he ne abood,
Toward his pauilons he rood.　　[1565] 1688

205   ¶ & otuwel a noon by-held,
    þere he rod in þe feld,
    & warende fore a non þo   *and tells the others.*
    Roulond & oliuer bo,   1692
    & ogger þat douȝty kniȝt,
    þat king garsie was tornd to fliȝt.
    þo roulond & oliuer,   *[fol. 277, back, col. 2.]*
    & þe gode kniȝt ogger,   1696
    Sien where king garsie rood,
    þer nas non þat lengere a-bood,
    Hasteliche þe wey þei nomen,   *They all pursue him.*
    & to king garsie þei comen.   1700

206   ¶ King garsie was a-fered to deye,
    & bi-gan mersi to crie,   *Garsie cries for mercy,*
    & seide, for soþe þat he wolde
    Of king charles, his lond holde,   1704
    & ben at eche parlement,
    Redi at his comaundement.

207   ¶ King garsie seide þis,
    " For his loue þat ȝoure good is,   1708
    Takeþ me on liue, & sle me nouȝt.
    Leet mi lif be for-bouȝt,
    & let me as a prisoun goon
    Bi-fore king charles a noon,   [1573] 1712
    & don him omage wiþ myn hon[d],   *and offers to do homage to Charles.*
    To holden of him al mi lond."

208   ¶ þanne seide otuwel,
    þat was douȝti kniȝt & snel,   1716
    To roulond & to oliuer,
    & to þe gode kniȝt ogger,
    " Nou he haueþ þis ȝift iȝiue,   *At Otuel's suggestion they*
    I rede þat we laten him liue.   1720 *spare his life,*
    Bi-fore þe king he schall be brouȝt,
    For gode, we nulle slen him nouȝt ; "

An þei acenteden þerto,
& seiden, " it wile be wel ido."   1724
& wiþ outen any targing,
þei ladden him bi-fore þe king.

209 ¶ þanne seide otuwel, þat gode kniȝt,
To king charles a non riȝt,   1728
" Sire," he seide, "her is garsie,
þat sumtime þratte þe to die,
He wile nou, ȝif þi wille be,
Do þe omage & feaute,   1732
& ben at þi comaundement ;
& at eche parlement,
Al redi at þin hond,
& holden of þe al his lond,   1736
& for his lond rente ȝiue,
Wiþ þe noue he mote liue."

*   *   *   *   *   *

[*End of MS.*]

NOTES.

p. 3, l. 23.   "be": by the time that: so in l. 38.

p. 4, l. 45.   "for the Rude lufe": for the love of the cross.

p. 4, l. 46.   "Rauf Coilȝear": that is Ralph the charcoal-burner.

p. 4, l. 50.   "Coilis": charcoal.

p. 5, l. 63.   St. Julian was the patron of travellers. Thus in the *Ancren Riwle*, p. 350: "Heo iuinded, iwis, sein Julianes in, þet weiuerinde men ȝeorne seched." Chaucer says of the Franklin that, "Seynt Julian he was in his contre." Prol. 340. See Mr. Furnivall's note in his edition of *Awdeley and Harman*, p. xxix; Dr. Morris' note on the passage quoted above from *Chaucer*, Chambers' *Book of Days*, II. 388; Brande, *Popular Antiquities*, ed. Hazlitt, I. 303, &c., and compare l. 973 below. In "John de Reeue," l. 170, the Reeve promises to give the king and his two companions lodging for the night, and adds

> "soo that yee take itt thankeffullye
> in gods name and *S^t. Iollye*,
> I aske noe other pay."

And again, l. 572, the guests when leaving on the following morning "thanked god & *S^t. Iollye*."

p. 5, l. 86.   "Pryse at the parting": that is, don't praise too soon or till the entertainment is over. The same expression occurs in the *Gesta Romanorum*, ch. xii. p. 39, l. 20, where the original Latin is *a fine laudatur opus*. See further in my note to the passage.

p. 6, l. 96.   I do not understand the word *chin*.

p. 7, l. 147.   "begin the buird": take the chief seat at the table. Compare *Chaucer C. T.*, Prol. 52. In "John de Reeue" the Reeve bids the king "begin the dish (dais)," and again, John when told to "begin the bord," "att the bords end he sate him downe," l. 824.

p. 9, l. 209.   Compare the supper provided by Iohn de Reeue for his guests:

> "By then came in red wine & ale
>   the bores head into the hall,
>   then sheild with sauces seere;
> Capons both baked and rosted,
> woodcockes, venison, without bost
>   & dish meeate dight ffull deere.
>
> Swannes they had piping hott,
> Coneys, curleys, well I wott,
>   the crane, the hearne, in ffcre,
> pigeons, partrid[g]es, with spiceryo,
> Elkes, ffloures, with ffrotrerye."

p. 11, l. 262.   "the ane": thee alone.

p. 12, l. 290.   He will, without doubt, be found to blame who is absent.

p. 12, l. 306.   "Peter!"   A common exclamation.   See Prof. Skeat's note to *P. Plowman*, C. viii. 182.

p. 14, l. 355.   "As the buik says."   See Introduction.

p. 14, l. 369.   "but ȝone man that ȝe knew,"&c., unless you know that man ; to put yourself at his disposal or mercy.

p. 15, l. 379.   "The fate will be mine alone."

p. 16, l. 436.   "Do way!"   So in *Guy of Warwick*, ed. Turnbull, 9844 : "*Do way*, leue sir, seyd Gij."

p. 18, l. 499.   "It might be set down to your harm."

p. 20, l. 537.   "me tharth": I need, þar = O.E. þearf, Ger. darf, was in Mid-English used both as a personal and impersonal verb.   Comp. "*the* þar not drede."   *Guy of Warwick*, l. 6770, and "Of no wepon *he* þar not dowte," *ibid.* l. 6830.

p. 20, l. 540.   I do not understand this line.

p. 23, l. 664.   "They thought the charcoal-burner hardly worth looking at."

p. 24, l. 681.   "bestiall" : one of the few words which appear to bear out the theory of a French origin of the poem.

p. 24, l. 693.   Read "Fra thir wyis, I-wis, to went on my way."

p. 26, l. 745.   "He has deserved that, in our opinion."

p. 26, l. 746.   "god forbot" : See *Cathol. Anglicum*, *s. v.* Forbott, p. 137, and note to *Sege of Melayne*, l. 406.

p. 27, l. 768.   "thy schone that thow wan."   See Prof. Zupitza's note to *Guy of Warwick*, l. 436.

p. 29, l. 835.   "Mait" : Fr. *mat*.   See *Sir Ferumbras* Glossary, and *Sege of Melayne*, note to l. 1284.

p. 30, l. 864.   "The lenth of ane rude braid."   Compare *Sir Ferumbras*, l. 971.

p. 30, l. 866.   "pithis" : see the *Catholicon*, *s. v.* Pythe, p. 282, and note.

p. 30, l. 888.   "that maist of michtis may" : a common expression in the old romances.

p. 32, l. 941.   "Angeris" : See the *Catholicon*, *s. v.*

p. 32, l. 955.   "caryit" : hastened.   See instances in note to *Roland and Otuel*, l. 1555.

p. 53, l. 973.   "sanct July" : see note to l. 63 above.

p. 39, l. 79.   "an heiȝeiug" : at once.   The same phrase occurs again, ll. 380, 501.

p. 39, l. 98, 99.   Probably these lines should be transposed : the meaning being, he besought him for the crown and the cross, on which Christ suffered death.

p. 40, l. 105.   Compare *Sir Ferumbras*, l. 5955.

p. 40, l. 106.   To feel was used of any of the senses not necessarily of touch.   Thus in *Gesta Romanorum*, p. 313, we read of hounds *feeling* a smell, as here.   See note to Fele in *Cathol. Anglicum*.

p. 40, l. 130. "longys": Longinus: see Prof. Skeat's note to *P. Plowman*, C. xxi. 82.

p. 41, l. 137. "at": of. Compare "he nom ráed *æt* his monnen." *Lazamon*, 1648, and "mai he no leue *at* here taken." *Genesis and Exodus*, 2697.

p. 41, l. 140. "he": that is Charles.

p. 41, l. 141. Here begins the life of Charles, written by the *Pseudo-Turpin*. "opon a niȝt": Lat. *per singular noctes sœpe perspiceret.*

p. 41, l. 154. For the construction, see Prof. Skeat's notes to *P. Plowman*, C. ix. 16, xvi. 131, and Prof. Zupitza's note to *Guy of Warwick*, l. 503, and *Sir Ferumbras*, l. 753, and note. Compare p. 93, l. 948 below.

p. 41, l. 155. "on þe se": Lat. *super mare Galileæ.*

p. 42, l. 173. "way of sterres": Lat. *caminum stellarum.*

p. 42, l. 188. "sex": Lat. *tribus.*

p. 43, l. 221. The *Pseudo-Turpin* gives the names as follows: "In Galletia, Visimia, Lamego, Dunia, Coimbria, Lirgo, Aurenias, Irattudo, Midonia, Buchara, (metropolis civitas sanctæ Mariæ,) Unarana, Crunia, Compostella: in Hispania, Auchala, Godolfaria, Taubamanca, Uzaeda, Ulmos, Canalias, Madriz, Marquada, Talavera: Medicina cœli, quæ est urbs excelsa: Berlanga, Osma, Seguntia, Segovia, quæ est Magna Avila, Salamanca, Sepulvega, Tolleta, Calatana, Badagotet, Eger, Godiano, Enuta, Altamora, Palencia, Lucena, Ventosa, quæ dicitur Carcesa, quæ est in valle viridi, Capana, Austega, Ovetum, Legio, Carrina, Duca, Nageras, Calacina, Urantia, Galathi, Miranda, Tutela, Sanagotia, quæ dicitur Cæsaraugusta, Pampilonia, Baiona, Iacca, Osca, in qua XC turres esse solent, Barbastra, Terragoa, Lerida, Tortosa oppidum fortissimum, Barbagalli oppidum fortissimum, Carmone op. fort., Aurelia, op. fort., Algaleti urbs, Adania, Inispalida, Excalona, Horamalagne . . . Satina, Granata, Sibilia, Corduba, Abula, Acintina in qua jacet beatus Torquatus Christi confessor, beati Jacobi cliens, ad sepulcrum cujus arbor olivæ divinitus florens miris fructibus onustatur per unumquemque annum in solemnitate ejusdem, ii. id. Madii." Caxton in his *Charles the Grete*, III. i. 2, judiciously omits the greater number.

p. 44, l. 264. "front": an evident mistake for fruit: see above, and compare Caxton: "whyche dyd bere rype fruyt."

p. 44, l. 271. "Portingale & lauers": Lat. *tellus Porto-gallorum, tellus Alavarum.*

p. 44, l. 272. "Landulof": Lat. *Alandalutiorum tellus:* "Chastel": *tellus Castellanorum.*

p. 44, l. 273. "Bigairs": Lat. *Biscaiorum tellus.* "Bastles": *tellus Basclorum.*

p. 44, l. 274. "Moys & nauers": Lat. *tellus Maurorum, tellus Navanorum.*

p. 44, l. 278. "tvelmoneþ": Lat. *trium mensium spatio.* Caxton: "foure monethes." Probably for *&* we should read *an.*

p. 45, l. 290.   Lat. *est inhabitata usque in hodiernum diem.*   In the Latin the names appear as *Lacena, Ventosa, Canina, Adania.*

p. 45, l. 294.   " ganbern " : the scribe appears to have mistaken these two words for one, as though there was another town " ganbern " ; the meaning of course is that Charles at the same time burnt the town of Lucerne.

p. 45, ll. 296-301.   The Latin only says : *quidam est gurges, qui a tribus annis in medio ejus* [Lucerne] *surrexit, in quo magni pisces et nigri habentur.*   Compare Caxton.

p. 45, l. 306.   " A fair miracle " : there is no reference to this in the *Pseudo-Turpin.*

p. 45, l. 314.   " And because they called so for baskets these men still call the city Paners, and will to the world's end."

p. 46, l. 317.   " Clodonius " : Lat. *Clodoveus.*

p. 46, l. 318.   " clotayis " : Lat. *Lotharius.*

p. 46, ll. 320-322.   Lat. partim *Hispaniam acquisiverant, partim dimiserunt, sed hic Carolus totam Hispaniam suis temporibus subjugavit.*

p. 46, l. 328.   See Introduction : and compare l. 429.

p. 46, l. 331.   " þe gilder lond " : Lat. *in terra Alandabuf,* and so Caxton.

p. 46, l. 332.   " salanicodus " : Lat. *Salameadis.   Cader dicitur proprie locus in quo est Salam, in lingua arabica Deus dicitur.*   Caxton : " Salancadys," which is the truest reading.

p. 47, l. 356.   Lat. *antistitem et canonicos secundum beati Isidori episcopi et confessoris regulam instituit.*

p. 47, l. 362.   " burdewes " : Lat. *apud urbem buturensem.*

p. 47, l. 363.   " anevaus " : Lat. *urben qua vulgo dicitur Axa.*

p. 47, l. 366.   " þre mones & fourten niȝt " : Caxton : " thre yere."

p. 47, l. 371.   " Sir romain " : Lat. *Romaricus.*

p. 47, l. 380.   " on heiȝeing " : see note to l. 79.

p. 47, l. 387.   " to hundred schillinges " : Lat. *centum solidis.*

p. 47, l. 388.   The subject (the false executor) is omitted.

p. 48, l. 389.   " þe nende " : = at then ende or atten ende, the end : compare *atte nale* = at the ale-house (*P. Plowman,* c. viii. 19). See Prof. Skeat's note to *P. Plowman,* c. i. 43.

p. 48, l. 396.   " in pin þat wel strong were " : Lat. *in tartareis pœnis.*

p. 48, l. 422.   See note to *Gesta Romanorum,* ch. liii. p. 372, l. 24.

p. 49, l. 425.   ll. 425-461 are not in the *Pseudo-Turpin :* their place being taken by a long account of the struggle between Charles and Aigoland, which is given by Caxton in his lyf of *Charles the Grete,* Bk. III., pt. i. ll. 5—10 inclusive, pp. 208-220, ed. 1880-1881

p. 49, l. 431.   *Caxton,* Bk. I., pt. ii. c. 3 (pp. 267, ed. 1880-1881) is rather vague, as he says " the lengthe of hys persone conteyned eyght feet after the mesure of his feet, which were merueyllously long "—and so the Latin.

p. 50, l. 464.   " nasers " : Lat. *Nageram.*

p. 50, l. 466. "Vernague": Lat. *Ferracutus*. Caxton: *Feragus;* one of "the generacion of golias."

p. 50, ll. 473, 474. The scribe has reversed the numbers, for in l. 473, for "tventi": Caxton reads, "fourty," and so the Latin; and in l. 474 the Lat. has *viginti*, and Caxton, "twelue cubytes."

p. 50, l. 476. Caxton says, "a cubyte brode," and so the Latin.

p. 51, l. 501. "an hey3eing": Lat. *illico:* Caxton, "without makyng' of ony semblaunte of warre."

p. 51, l. 509. "Reynald de aubeþpine": Lat. *Rainadas de albo spino:* Caxton, "Raynold daulbepyn."

p. 51, l. 518. According to the Latin it was *Constantinus, rex romanus et Oliverius comes* that were next sent out to oppose Vernagu: Caxton gives the names as "Constayn of Rome & therte Noel."

p. 51, l. 525. A common expression: compare "al so stille als a ston." *Havelok*, 928. See also *Otuel*, l. 1641.

p. 51, l. 537. Compare *Sir Ferumbras*, l. 521 and note.

p. 51, l. 560. See note to *Sir Ferumbras*, l. 988, and Dr. Hausknecht's note to the *Sowdone of Babylone*, l. 875.

p. 51, l. 564. He knew of no better help or resource.

p. 53, l. 581. "to þe neue": to the evening: Lat. *usque ad nonam*. See note to l. 389 above.

p. 53, l. 585. There is no mention in either the original Latin or Caxton of an agreement that Roland was to be armed with a staff instead of a sword.

p. 53, l. 588. The pronoun when the subject is frequently omitted: see Prof. Zupitza's note to *Guy of Warwick*, l. 10.

p. 53, l. 593. "a staf": &c., Lat. *baculum quemdam retortum et lignum* (read *longum*) *secum detulit*.

p. 54, l. 612. "asleped": compare *Sir Bevys*, 1697:

> "He wex *asleped* wonder sore,
> He mighte ride no forther more:
> He reinede his hors to a chesteine,
> And felle aslepe vpon the pleine."

p. 54, l. 684. "To redeem that which was lost."

p. 54, l. 685. A common simile in mediæval theological writers.

p. 57, l. 738. See note to l. 154 above.

p. 59, l. 795. "fot hot": on the spot, instantly, hastily. Compare Chaucer, *Man of Lawes Tale*, 438: "Custance han thy take anon, *foot-hot*." The form *hot-fot*, with the same meaning, occurs in the *Debate of the Body and Soul*, l. 481, and *full-hote* in *Guy of Warwick*, 5063, 6498, 6656, &c.

p. 60, l. 826. See note to l. 795.

p. 60, l. 855. "me": no doubt a mistake for "be."

p. 61, l. 861. "brust": apparently the only instance of this form.

p. 61, l. 872. "a": on, in.

p. 61, l. 874. Perhaps we should insert & before miri: "with salve! and merry song."

p. 61, l. 878.   See Introduction.

p. 66, l. 52.   "gynges": nations, peoples.   A.S. *genge*, Icel. *gengi*.

p. 66, l. 55.   "childermasse day."   See Introduction, p. xiii, and note to *Roland and Otuel*, l. 686.

p. 68, l. 103.   "Hit": so in *Sir Ferumbras*, ll. 1981, 3114, 3183, it is used referring to males, even in the plural.

p. 68, l. 109.   "þou art a-boute": thou art trying.   See the *Catholicon Anglicum*, *s. v.* to Beabowteward, and additional note, p. xxviii.

p. 68, l. 120.   "te": the same form occurs again, l. 302.

p. 69, l. 135.   "kypte": seized, caught up.   Icel. *kippa*.

p. 69, l. 136.   Probably we should read either "a muche gret fir brond," or "a gret muchel fir brond."

p. 70, l. 176.   "it him bar": I do not exactly understand these words.

p. 70, l. 182.   See Prof. Zupitza's note to *Guy of Warwick*, 6579.

p. 70, l. 184.   The meaning is that he would give him the tonsure with his sword in such a manner that he would never be able to receive it from any bishop.

p. 71, l. 192.   Compare "al nas wurþ an hawe."   *Robert of Gloucester*, p. 524.   For similar expressions see note to *Sir Ferumbras*, l. 5442.

p. 72, l. 227.   "Holte o roum": stand off, keep your distance.   So in the *Towneley Mysteries*, p. 235: "stand on roume."

p. 72, l. 231.   "all & some": fully, completely.

p. 72, l. 239.   Compare *Sir Ferumbras*, l. 1808, and note.

p. 72, l. 251.   The sone of the king of Armenia: see note to p. 41, l. 154.

p. 72, l. 280.   "Thought so little of them."

p. 73, l. 290.   "ʒef ich may": as far as lies in my power.   The phrase occurs frequently in *Guy of Warwick:* see the editor's note to l. 983.

p. 74, l. 308.   There is evidently some corruption here, though the meaning is plain enough.

p. 74, l. 319.   The forms *ich* and *ihc* are used indiscriminately in this poem.

p. 76, l. 325.   "Cristes cors" comes strangely from the lips of a Saracen.

p. 76, l. 340.   See note to p. 41, l. 154; and note to *Roland and Otuel*, l. 313.

p. 76, l. 348.   See note to l. 290, above.

p. 77, l. 377.   "slep": this strong form of the verb is not unusual; see instances in Stratmann.

p. 77, l. 384.   See note to l. 103.

p. 78, l. 394.   "For": in order that.

p. 78, l. 400.   "houinge": see Prof. Zupitza's note to *Guy of Warwick* 6338.

p. 78, l. 437.   "nekste:" nearest, shortest.

p. 78, l. 447.   "steue": strong, stiff.   The word is not common.

p. 79, l. 466.   See note to l. 400.

p. 79, l. 476.   Evidently there is a corruption here.

p. 79, 1 485.   See Prof. Zupitza's note to *Guy of Warwick*, l. 6579.

p. 79, l. 491.   See note to p. 51, l. 525.

p. 79, l. 495.   " so mote ich þe ": as I may thrive.   An expression of very frequent occurrence.   See Prof. Zupitza's note to *Guy of Warwick*, l. 615.

p. 80, l. 517.   " nese ": here, equal to cousin : nephew and niece were used, like cousin, vaguely for different degrees of relationship.   See *Catholicon Anglicum, s. vv. Nese* and *Nevowe*.

p. 80, ll. 523, 530.   See note to *Sir Ferumbras*, l. 408.

p. 80, l. 529.   " beie ": both.   So in *Robert of Gloucester*, 47.   " þat . . . ȝonge were *beie*."

p. 80, ll. 595, 596.   That word pleased Roland well, and he answered Otuel: on the omission of the subject pronoun compare p. 51, l. 588, above, and *Sege of Melayne*, l. 27.

p. 83, l. 603.   " loþ ": here seems to mean enmity, but the general meaning is hurt, injury.

p. 83, l. 605.   They embraced and kissed each other, as if each had been the other's brother.

p. 83, l. 612.   What has happened to you and this man ?

p. 83, l. 631.   The subject pronoun þei is omitted.

p. 84, l. 638.   " nammo " = no more, no others.   Cf. l. 1334.

p. 84, l. 640.   And had become reconciled to the king.

p. 84, l. 661.   Compare the corresponding passage in *Roland and Otuel*, l. 671.

p. 85, l. 677.   " Averil was comen & winter gon ":   In *Roland and Otuel*, " one þe forthirmoste daye of auerille," l. 721.

p. 86, l. 717.   "Turabeles": called in l. 769, below, *Curabiles*, and in *Roland and Otuel*, l. 785, *Corsabill*, and in l. 817, *Corsabolyn*.

p. 87, l. 742.   "Daþeit": an interjection or imprecation with the meaning of curses on ! cursed ! ill betide !   It occurs frequently in Mid. English romances, &c.   See for instance *Sir Tristram*, pp. 111, 191 ; *Havelok*, 296, 300, 926, &c. ; *Horn Childe*, p. 290 ; *Seven Sages*, 2395 ; *Owl and Nightingale*, l. 99, &c.   With the line compare *Macbeth*, v. 7 : " Damned be him that first cries, hold, enough ! " and l. 1182, below.

p. 87, l. 752.   Perhaps we should read " it is."

p. 88, l. 792.   " & ": this is frequently used throughout the poem, in the sense of *but :* compare l. 837.

p. 89, l. 828.   Compare the *Sowdone of Babylone*, l. 1163 : " Thai *worthed* vp on here stedes."

p. 90, l. 867.   " were at on ": agreed ; were of one mind.

p. 91, l. 891.   " markeden ": signed with the cross.

p. 91, l. 904.   " þef ": commonly used as a title of opprobrium or contempt.

p. 92, l. 926.   "du3e peers:" See note to *Sir Ferumbras*, l. 197. Here the meaning appears simply to be a chosen knight.

p. 93, l. 948.   "On of kinges kni3tes garsie": one of the knights of King Garsie.   See note to p. 41, l. 154.   Compare l. 1000.

p. 93, l. 980.   See note to l. 290, above.

p. 94, l. 1000.   See note to l. 948.

p. 94, l. 1001.   "3o": the same form occurs in the *Ormulum*, 115; *Polit. Religious and Love Songs*, iii. 79 and 84.

p. 95, l. 1032.   Compare *Sir Ferumbras*, 5127, "w3t þat þe selue, syr Amyrant": and the *Sege of Melayne*, ll. 555 and 698, and *Song of Roland*, l. 638.

p. 96, l. 1065.   We know not what has become of him.   See Prof. Skeat's note to *P. Plowman*, B. v. 651.

p. 99, l. 1161.   "I will make peace or reconciliation for that in which you have offended against Garsie."

p. 100, l. 1182.   Compare l. 742, and note.

p. 100, l. 1201.   For "þe" read "þe[i]."   "at on": agreed, of one mind.   See Prof. Zupitza's note to *Guy of Warwick*, l. 5308.

p. 103, l. 1307.   "so mote ich go": a phrase of frequent occurrence in the old romances.   See numerous instances in Prof. Zupitza's note to *Guy of Warwick*, l. 2572.

p. 104, l. 1320.   as a sign of business or profession of a barber-surgeon.

p. 106, l. 1408.   "le": apparently inserted by the translator inadvertently.

p. 109, ll. 1505-1508.   Compare ll. 1555-1558.

p. 112, l. 1588.   "gunde": a curious form, being really a double preterite.

p. 112, l. 1619.   "Til": while.

p. 113, l. 1645.   "And he pushed the window open, so that it flew all to pieces."

p. 114, l. 1673.   "Fous": probably we should read *fresch* or *frechs*. Cf. ll. 1059 & 1439.

p. 114, l. 1680.   I do not quite understand this line.

p. 114, l. 1710.   So in *Ayenbite*, p. 78: "hi couþen hire zennen vorbegge."

GLOSSARIAL INDEX.

Bair, 28/801, *adj.* open ; 17/457, *vb. pt. t.* wore, bare; 9/187, *sb.* wild boar

Bakheir, 29/848, *sb.* supporter, backer, second

Bald, 15/409, *sb.* bold, daring man

Bancouris, 24/685, *sb. pl.* coverings for benches

Band, 28/800, *vb. pt. s.* bound, tied

Bandis, 23/631, *sb. pl.* bolts, fastenings

Bane, 16/422, *adj.* ready

Banis, 17/474, *sb. pl.* bones

Basnet, 17/484, *sb.* small helmet, O.Fr. *bassinet*, dimin. of *bassin* = a helmet in the shape of a *basin*

Batteris, 30/886, *vb. imper.* fight, strike

Bayne, 22/608, *adv.* readily, actively

Be, 15/385, *adv.* before, by the time that

Becum, 31/893, *vb. imper.* become

Beed, 84/641, *v. pt. s.* offered

Beget, 22/607, *vb.* deceive

Begouth, 6/120, *vb. pt. t.* began, was about to

Begylit, 25/713, *pp.* deceived, tricked

Behufe, 4/41, *sb.* advantage, benefit

Beie, 80/529, *a.* both

Beir, 12/289, *vb.* hold

Beird, 8/177, *vb. pt. t.* roared, shouted. A.S. (ge)-*bæran*

Beirnis, 9/189, *sb. pl.* people, lit. children. Sc. *bairns*

Beliue, 6/94, *adv.* quickly, at once. O.E. *bi life* = with life

Bellisand, 18/478, *adj.* elegant. Fr. *belle*, used adverbially, and *seant* = becoming

Bennysoun, 9/214, *sb.* blessing, benison

Bent, 26/733, *sb.* moor, heath. Ger. *binse* = rush, *bent* grass

Benwart, 7/131, *adv.* inwards, towards the interior of the house

Beriall, 17/465, *sb.* beryl

Bestiall, 24/681, *sb.* animals, cattle. Fr. *bestiall*

Bet, 7/144, *pp.* made better, made up. A.S. *bétan*

Betakin, 15/405, *vb.* mean, betoken

Betaucht, 27/775, *sb.* committed, given in charge. A.S. *bitæcan*

Betuix, 14/344, *prep.* between. A.S. *betweox*

Bid, 13/315, *vb. pr. t.* desire, wish

Biddeth, 82/568, *imp. pl.* pray, beg

Bigge, 56/684, *v.* to buy, redeem

Bigging, 9/190, *sb.* house, building

Bileue, 91/1132, *v.* leave off

Birny, 27/767, *sb.* corslet

Blan, 28/825, *vb. pt. t.* ceased, stopped. A.S. *blinnan*

Bland, 20/565, *sb.* engagement ; probably an error for *band*

Blandit, 17/475, *pp.* blended, mixed

Blenkit, 29/854, *vb. pt. t.* glanced, looked

Blenkt, 78/460, *v. pt. s.* gave away

Bleue, 74/320, *v.* remain, abide

Blin, 6/92, *vb.* stop, rest

Bliue, 95/1035, *adv.* quickly

Blonk, 28/800, *sb.* steed. Planchaz, *equus pallidus hodie blank.* Schilter. Thus *blonk* may have originally meant merely a *white* horse. Fr. *blanc* cheval.—Jamieson.

Blyth, 5/75, *adj.* pleased, glad

Bocht, 8/182, *vb. pt. t.* bought, redeemed

Bode, 38/52, *s.* message

Bodword, 31/905, *sb.* warning

Boist, 14/371, *sb.* threatening, abuse; 30/885, *sb.* boasting, boasts

Boistit, 27/784, *vb. pt. t.* boasted

Bone, 59/807, *s.* a prayer, a petition

Bordourit, 17/464, *pp.* bordered, encircled

Borwe, 74/305, *s.* a security. *Finde Mahoun to borwe* = bring Mahomet as my security

Bot gif, 20/551, unless

Boun, 7/124, *adj.* ready. Icel. *buuin,* pp. of *bua* = to prepare; 16/425, *vb.* get ready, prepare

Bowre, 19/535, *s.* palace, chamber. A.S. *búr*

Braid, 30/861, *sb.* stroke; 28/810, *adj.* broad; 4/34, around, about

Braidit, 30/867, *vb. pt. t.* drew. A.S. *bredan*

Braissaris, 17/473, *sb. pl.* vambraces. In ancient armour pieces between the elbow and the top of the shoulder, fastened together by straps inside the arms. Fr. *brassard, brassart*

Braissit, 20/553, *pp.* enveloped, covered. Fr. [em]*brasser*

Braithlie 8/177, *adv.* violently, loudly

Brand, 19/520, *sb.* sword. A.S. *brand, brond*

Brandis, 7/131, *sb. pl.* brands, logs of wood

Braun, 9/187, *sb.* brawn

Breid, 8/154, *sb.* breadth, width; 9/187, *sb.* bread

Brent, 28/800, *adj.* steep

Brief, 30/885, *vb. imper.* [?]

Broun, 28/800, *sb. pl.* rising ground, hill

Browdin, 24/685, *pp.* embroidered

Browis, 30/862, *sb. pl.* brows. A.S. *brúa,* pl. of *brú*

Brust, 61/861, *s.* a bristle

Buird, 7/147, *sb.* the board or table, hence = meal. A.S. *bord*

Buklair, 19/519, *sb.* buckler

Burelie, 9/190, *adj.* rough, rustic

Burneist, 17/464, *pp.* burnished, polished. Fr. *brunir*

Busk, 28/800, *sb.* bush, small tree

Busked, 39/83; Buskit, 15/409, *vb. pt. t.* got ready, prepared. Icel. *buask* = to prepare oneself, from *bua* = to prepare

Busteous, 26/733, *adj.* rough, burly. Welsh *bwyst*

Busteously, 21/596, *adv.* roughly

Byde, 27/784, *vb.* meet, await

Bynome, 90/848, *pp.* taken away from

Byrd, 8/162, *impers. vb.* it behoved, it became

Byrdis, 19/536, *sb. pl.* ladies; 9/211, *sb. pl.* birds, fowls

Byre, 6/111, *sb.* cowhouse

Byrnand, 7/132, *pr. p.* burning. AS. *brennan*

Cachit, 4/33, *vb. pt. t.* wandered, went astray. O.Fr. *cachier*

Call, 23/640, *vb.* drive away

Can, 22/624, *vb. pr. t.* knows; 25/703, *vb. pt. t.* began

Cant, 4/42, *adj.* lively, active

Cantlie, 15/388, *adv.* actively, briskly

Capill, 4/43, *sb.* horse. Lat. *caballus*

Carll, 4/42, *sb.* churl, countryman. A.S. *ceorl*

Carpit, 4/44, *vb. pt. t.* spoke. Cf. Eng. *chirp*

Carpit, 24/683, *pp.* carpeted

Cassin, 22/616, *pr. p.* cast off, broken

Cast, 4/33, *sb.* lot, chance

Catchit, 15/384, *vb. pt. t.* started, hastened

Caucht, 15/384, *vb. pt. t.* threw up, placed; 29/841, tried, wished

Chachand, 4/42, *pr. p.* chachand the gait = pursuing his course. O.Fr. *chachier*

Chaip, 20/561, *vb.* escape. Fr. *eschapper*

Chalmer, 27/774, *sb.* chamber

Chauffray, 13/323, *sb.* merchandise

Cheiftyme, 3/1, *sb.* reign

Cheir, 8/180, *sb.* welcome; 29/843, mien

Cheualrous, 29/843, *adj.* chivalrous, knightly

Cheueris, 5/96, *vb. pr. t.* shiver

Childermasse day, 66/55, *sb.* the Holy Innocents' Day

Chin, 5/96, *sb.* [?]

Circulit, 18/477, *pp.* encircled, set round

Clais, 16/434, *sb. pl.* clothes, dress

Cled, 24/683, *pp.* covered

Cleikit, 28/823, *vb. pt. t.* snatched. A.S. *gelæccan;* cf. Eng. *clutch*

Cleir, 18/497, *adj.* pure, spotless

Clene, 7/125, *adv.* completely, quite

Clippe, 83/605, *vb.* embrace

Clois, 27/776, *adj.* close-fitting

Closand, 24/684, *pr. p.* closing in, fitting

Coft, 6/105, *pp.* bought. Ger. *kaufen* = to buy

Coillis, 4/50, *sb. pl.* coals, that is, charcoal

Columbyn, 24/674, *sb.* columbine

Commounis, 16/431, *sb. pl.* common people

Compeir, 9/200, *vb.* appear

Conseruit, 32/946, *vb. pt. t.* established

Conuert, 31/894, *vb.* be converted

Cop, 9/214, *sb.* cup, glass

Cornellis, 24/684, *sb. pl.* corners

Counsingis, 31/900, *sb. pl.* relations

Counteris, 30/875, *vb. pr. t.* encounter, contend

Coursour, 6/115, *sb.* steed

Courtes, 25/719, *adj.* courteous

Courtingis, 11/267, *sb. pl.* curtains. O.Fr. *curtine, cortine*

Couth, 7/125, *vb. pt. t.* didst know, understood. A.S. *cunnan,* pt. t. *ic. cuðe*

Crabitnes, 19/528, *sb.* quarrelling, ill-temper

Craue, 18/498, *vb.* ask. Be to craue = be a question of asking

Creillis, 4/43, *sb. pl.* panniers, baskets, creels

Cristallis, 17/475, *sb. pl.* crystals

Crouste, 93/954, *sb.* crust

Cule, 29/841, *vb.* cool

Cumlie, 9/196, *adv.* courteously

Cunnand, 8/165, *adj.* sensible; 13/321, *sb.* covenant, promise

Cunning, 6/93, *sb.* knowledge

Cunningis, 9/209, *sb. pl.* rabbits

Cuplit, 4/43, *pp.* coupled, tied together

Cusingis, 31/916, *sb. pl.* friends. *See* Counsingis

Cussanis, 17/472, *sb. pl.* armour for the thighs

Daillis, 15/385, *sb. pl.* dales

Dantely, 24/667, *adv.* daintily

Dantit, 16/435, *pp.* frightened, daunted. O.Fr. *danter.* Lat. *domitare*

Dawin, 15/385, *pr. p.* dawning, breaking

Daynteis, 9/191, *sb. pl.* dainties, delicacies

Debait, 4/44, *sb.* hesitation, delay

Defend, 5/60, *vb. pr. t.* forbid, object

Deill, 19/514, *vb.* deal, give

Deip, 3/17, *sb.* [?]

Deir, 11/254, *adv.* dearly ; 19/515, *adj.* wild

Deis, 9/191, *sb.* table. Fr. *dais*

Deme, 24/677, *vb.* examine

Dentit, 24/667, *pp.* set, inlaid

Derf, 15/385, *adj.* bold, hardy

Derfly, 28/798, *adv.* boldly

Deuise, 22/614, *vb. pr. t.* say, tell

Dew, 14/365, *vb. pt. t.* dawned. A.S. *dagian*

Dicht, 7/133, *vb.* prepare, get ready

Digne, 14/354, *adj.* worthy, noble

Ding, 31/918, *vb.* strike, smite

Discouerand, 28/798, *pr. p.* exploring

Dispair, 32/933, *adj.* unequal, unsuitable

Dispittously, 31/904, *adv.* despitefully

Disseuer, 19/527, *vb.* separate, part

Docht, 27/792, *vb. pt. t.* could, was able

Dois, 5/86, *vb. pr. t.* farest

Dosouris, 24/676, *sb. pl.* canopies

Douchereis, 32/926, *sb. pl.* duchies

Douchtie, 21/590, *adj.* valiant, doughty man. A.S. *dohtig*

Dourly, 31/918, *adv.* hardily, sternly

Draif, 3/17, *vb. pt. t.* drove

Dreichlie, 10/217, *adj.* slowly, as denoting long continuance (Jamieson)

Drest, 9/201, *pp.* treated

Drichtine, 29/856, *sb.* Our Lord. A.S. *drichten*

Drupe, 78/444, *a.* dry. Probably we should read druȝe or druþe

Dubbit, 26/755, *vb. pt. t.* dubbed, created

Duchepeiris, 3/10, *sb. pl.* the douzepers, or twelve Peers of Charlemagne

Dule, 9/201, *sb.* sorrow, mourning

Durandlie, 3/17, *adv.* continually, without intermission

Duris, 24/677, *sb. pl.* doors

Dwelling, 10/239, *sb.* absence, delay

Dyamountis, 17/466, *sb. pl.* diamonds

Dyntis, 13/514, *sb. pl.* blows

E, 24/695, *sb.* eye, attention

Eem, 75/341, *s.* uncle

Eie, 69/124, *v.* fear, dread, awe

Eir, 7/152, *sb.* ear

Eird, 8/156, *sb.* ground, floor

Eis, 16/222, *sb.* ease, comfort

Eismentis, 5/82, *sb. pl.* comforts

Ellis, 7/127, *adv.* otherwise, else

Enbraissit, 23/631, *vb. pt. t.* opened, undid

Enchaip, 13/318, *vb.* *See* note.

Encheef, 13/308, *vb.* achieve, accomplish, succeed

Engreif, 22/619, *vb.* be displeasing, annoy

Engreuit, 22/603, *pp.* vexed, annoyed

Erd, 43/215, *s.* a country, district

Errore, 79/489, *a.* former, previous

Eye, 68/101, *s.* fear, dread, awe

Failȝe, 29/835, *vb. pt. t.* fell, fainted

Faind, 8/155, *vb. pt. t.* feigned, pretended

Faindes, 31/902, *vb. pr. t.* pretend, feign

Fair, 6/112, *sb.* fare, food; 12/286, *vb.* to travel, journey; 16/419, *sb.* accompaniments, baggage

Fairand, 17/445, *pr. p.* travelling

Fairlie, 8/176, *adj.* wonderfully

Fais, 26/754, *sb.* faith, truth

Fallow, 5/72, *sb.* fellow, companion

Fand, 5/72, *vb. pt. t.* found, met

Fane, 9/207, *adj.* glad

Farne, 6/108, *pp.* fared

Fay, 5/88, *sb.* faith, truth

Fechand, 19/508, *pr. p.* fetching, carrying

Fechtine, 5/61, *sb.* quarrelling

Fechting, 17/463, *sb.* battles, fighting

Fee, 27/777, *sb.* property. Lat. *pecus*

Feerd, 90/839, *s.* company, troop

Feid, 33/969, *sb.* anger, enmity. Eng. *feud*

Feildis, 3/8, *sb. pl.* fields

Feir, 8/176, *sb.* fear

Feir, 10/220, in feir or into feir = together, in company

Feirslie, 3/18, *adv.* fiercely

Feld, 6/97, *vb. pt. t.* felt, experienced; 40/106, perceived, experienced

Fell, 3/2, *vb. pt. t.* happened, occurred

Fellis, 3/2, *sb.* wild and rocky hills

Fellonar, 28/813, *adj.* fiercer

Fellounlie, 3/18, *adv.* fiercely, wildly

Fensabill, 13/329, *adj.* fighting, sufficient for defence

Ferche, 96/105, *a.*; 107/1439, fresh. A.S. *fersc*

Ferd, 91/874, 105/1374, a company, a troop

Ferd, 108/1463, *s.* fear; 95/1042, *s.* ford

Ferly, 15/404, *sb.* wonder, astonishment

Ferlyfull, 3/2, *adj.* wonderful, fearful

Fet, 17/445, *vb.* fetch, procure

Fewaill, 10/244, *sb.* fuel

Fewtir, 28/812, *sb.* a rest for a spear

Fischis, 24/682, *sb. pl* fishes

Flamand, 24/671, *adj.* sparkling

Flan, 3/2, *sb.* storm, tempest. Icel. *flana*

Fleichingis, 31/902, *sb. pl.* flattering promises

Flem, 38/33, *v. t.* to banish, to drive out

Flourdelycis, 24/670, *sb. pl.* fleur-de-lis

Flure, 24/683, *sb.* floor

Follaut, 74/316, *s.*; follauȝt, 84/639, Baptism

Follede, 84/638, *v. pt. s.* baptised

Forbot, 26/746, *vb. impr.* forbid

For-bouȝt, 115/1710, *pa. par.* ransomed, redeemed

Forcenes, 28/814, *sb.*; forcynes, 28/820, fierceness

Ford, 26/734, *sb.* way, road

Forestaris, 9/197, *sb. pl.* foresters, keepers

Grassum, 32/939, *sb.* compensation, reward : lit. "the sum paid to a landlord by a tenant, at the entry of a lease, or by a new heir to a lease or feu" (Jamieson). A.S. *gærsuma* = compensation

Grauit, 17/457, *adj.* carved

Gre, 18/485, *sb.* prize, superiority

Greis, 17/471, *sb.* greaves

Grief, 13/314, *vb.* trouble, vex

Gromis, 27/787, *sb. pl.* men

Gudlie, 6/118, *adj.* kindly

Gyde, 25/720, *sb.* attire, dress

Gye, 66/40, *vb.* rule, govern

Gynges, 66/52, *sb. pl.* peoples

Gyrd, 7/151, *sb.* a stroke, blow

Haiket, 23/644, *vb. pt. t.* walked slowly, sauntered

Haill, 15/411, *adj.* whole

Hailsum, 24/675, *adj.* becoming, noble

Hair, 16/421, *adj.* cold, keen

Haist, 20/550, *vb.* haste, hurry

Haistely, 28/826, *adv.* hastily

Hald, 3/19, *vb.* hold, keep

Hale, 4/52, *adj.* whole, entire

Halely, 31/896, *adv.* wholly, entirely

Hamelie, 6/112, *adj.* homely, poor

Happin, 13/332, *vb.* happen upon, fall in with

Harberie, 4/41 ; harbery, 5/64, *sb.* refuge

Harbreit, 25/710, *vb. pt. t.* lodged

Hard, 12/282, *vb. pt. t.* heard

Harnes, 15/395, *sb.* arms, accoutrements

Harnest, 29/833, *adj.* armed, in armour

Hartfully, 30/891, *adv.* heartily, with the whole heart

Hecht, 15/382, *pp.* promised

Hechtis, 15/411, *sb. pl.* orders, engagements

Heet, 91/904, *v. pt. s.* was named

Heich, 3/19, *adv.* high, steep

Heid, 29/834, *sb.* heat : heuy with heid = oppressed with the heat

Heill, 20/567, *sb.* health : haldin in heill = in possession of good health .

Heip, 5/83 [?]

Heir, 5/72, *adv.* here

Heiȝeing, 39/79, *sb.* hurrying, haste : an heiȝeing = at once, in haste, without delay

Helf, 12/304, *sb.* assist, help

Hende, 33/970, *adj.* noble, gentle, kind

Here, 91/897, *sb.* company, troop

Hes, 5/81, *vb. pr. t.* hast

Het, 6/109, *adj.* hot

Heterliche, 81/559, *adv.* fiercely

Hew, 20/553, *sb.* colour

Hicht, 4/37, *sb.* on hicht = on high, lofty ; 18/496, height : the day may haue the *hicht* = may reach its turning-point, i. e. *noon*

Hie mes, 21/575, High mass

Hine, 29/857, *adv.* hence : "sall neuer hine" is equivalent to "shall never leave, or depart"

Holtis, 16/421, *sb. pl.* high, barren ground

Houe, 21/577, *sb.* delay

Houerit, 16/417, *vb. pt. t.* waited about

Huifis, 18/495, *vb. pr. t.* tarry, delay

Huit, 16/417, *sb. pt. t.* paused, stopped : the same as *houed*

Husband, 21/595, *adj.* ; 22/599, *sb.* farmer's, country

K 2

Ling, 16/428, *sb.* line : in ane
ling = in one line, that is, straight
on without stopping; 15/397,
heath, moor

Lofe, 4/45, *sb.* love; 5/87, *vb.*
praise

Lois, 23/642, *vb.* lose

Louȝ, 74/291, *vb. pt. s.* laughed

Ludgeit, 26/743, *pp.* lugged,
dragged

Lufesumly, 20/589, *adv.* plea-
santly

Luþer, 93/942, *adv.* bad, danger-
ous

Lyft, 13/326, *sb.* firmament, sky

Lykand, 4/40, *adj.* pleased, satisfied

Lykis, 32/943, *vb. pr. t.* pleases

Lykit, 4/39, *vb. pt. t.* pleased

Lystinit, 26/742, *vb. pt. t.* lis-
tened

Magre, 18/487, *sb.* difficulty

Maid, 6/121, *vb. pt. t.* caused

Maisterfull, 17/444, *adj.* powerful

Mait, 22/835, *adj.* fatigued. See
Glossary to *Sir Ferumbras, s. v.* Mat

Mantene, 29/853, *vb.* maintain,
support

Marschellit, 5/186, *pp.* arranged

Mat, 19/513, *vb.* annoy, interfere
with

Matchit, 9/186, *pp.* paired

Maumetes, 46/323, *sb. pl.* idols

Maumetrie, 65/25, *sb.* idolatry

May, 82/591, *sb.* a maid ; 30/
888, *vb. pr. t.* can do, is powerful

Meiknes, 26/655, *sb.* modesty

Meit, 5/81, *sb.* food, meat

Meitis, 15/397, *vb. pr. t.* meet

Mend, 32/957, *vb.* increase, aug-
ment

Mene, 6/121, *vb.* to complain

Mer, 3/22, *vb. pt. t.* put them
into confusion

Mettaill, 29/830, *sb.* mettle, ex-
cellence

Midmorne, 4/29, *sb.* the middle
of the morning

Mirrie, 7/137, *adj.* merry, pleasant

Mocht, 18/492, *aux. vb.* might

Mon, 16/427, *vb. pr. t.* must

Mote, 4/53, *aux. vb.* may

Mounde, 60/853, *sb.* power, lit.
protection. "A knight of mochel
mounde."—Launfal, 597. A.S.
mund

Mure, 3/14, *sb.* moor, heath

Myrk, 3/22, *adj.* dark, murky

Myster, 26/751, *sb.* desire, need ;
17/444, science, craft, art

Nait, 5/61, *sb.* need

Namit, 18/505, *vb. pt. t.* named,
mentioned by name

Nanis, 17/471, *adv.* for the nanis
= for the occasion, for the nonce

Neidlingis, 15/407, *adv.* needs, of
necessity

Nende, 48/389, *sb.* end. þe
nende = þen ende = the end

Neue, 53/581, *sb.* eve. þe *neue*
= þen eue = the eve. *Compare*
Nende

New, 20/547, *vb.* renew

Newlingis, 33/965, *adv.* recently,
lately

Nichtit, 4/40, *vb. pt. t.* became
night, or dark

Non, 53/602, *adj.* none; 14/344,
sb. noon

Noy, 20/538, *sb.* annoyance, hin-
drance

Nurtour, 8/162, *sb.* education,
manners

Nyse, 16/430, *adj.* foolish, silly

Raith, 20/551, *adv.* quickly, soon

Rauvingis, 31/898, *sb. pl.* ravings, foolish words

Red, 12/286, *vb. pr. t.* advise, recommend

Red, 11/261, *sb.* advice

Reddyit, 27/781, *vb. pt. t.* prepared, made ready

Regaird, 23/654, *sb.* notice, attention : countit at regaird = thought worth notice

Rek, 31/898, *vb. pr. t.* reckon, think, value

Remeid, 19/512, *sb.* remedy, satisfaction

Remufe, 20/864, *sb.* move, give away

Renk, 10/551, *sb.* way, course

Renkis, 28/822, *sb. pl.* strong men

Repreif, 29/846, *vb. pr. t.* reprove, blame

Restles, 28/822, *adj.* eager

Reuest, 14/346, *pp.* clothed, arrayed

Reulit, 17/468, *pp.* arranged ; 24/672, *pp.* painted, marked

Rew, 14/353, *sb.* street ; 23/551, *vb.* rue, repent

Reward, 23/652, *sb.* regard, attention

Rid, 38/891, *vb. pr. t.* advise, counsel

Rob, 21/578, *sb.* robe

Rois, 24/673, *sb.* roses

Ronsy, 18/481, *sb.* a hack, riding horse

Rot, 55/652, *vb. pt. t.* snored

Roustie, 19/520, *adj.* rusty

Rout, 54/629, *vb. pt. t.* snored. A.S. *hrútan*

Rouȝten, 14/1004, *vb. pt. pl.* recked, cared

Rowme, 28/812, *sb.* a spot, or place

Rubeis, 17/467, *sb. pl.* rubies

Rude, 4/45, *sb.* the cross

Rufe, 5/80, *sb.* rest, ease ; 6/109, *adj.* rough ; 24/672, roof, ceiling

Runsy, 28/794, *sb.* a hack, riding horse. *See* Ronsy

Rusit, 18/483, *vb. pt. t.* wondered, admired

Ryall, 3/14, *adj.* royal person, *i. e.* king

Ryally, 24/673, *adv.* royally

Ryfe, 8/172, *adj.* plentiful

Sa, 3/8, *adv.* so

Sadly, 23/658, *adv.* firmly, steadily

Saill, 10/245, *sb.* sale, market ; 25/716, *sb.* hall, saloon

Saird, 23/658, *vb. pt. t.* hurt

Salbe, 4/56, shall be

Salust, 16/424, *vb. pt. t.* saluted

Sapheir, 17/466, *sb.* sapphires

Sayand, 5/77, *pr. p.* saying

Scant, 11/275, *sb.* lack, need

Schapin, 17/461, *pp.* shaped

Scheild, 17/461, *sb.* shield

Schene, 17/461, *adj.* shining, glittering

Schill, 5/59, *adj.* chill, cold

Schir, 4/44, *sb.* sir

Schone, 27/768, *sb. pl.* lit. shoes, here = spurs

Schord, 26/736, *vb. pt. t.* threatened, scolded, abused

Schow, 25/700, *sb.* shove, push

Schroud, 17/461, *pp.* covered, protected

Seigis, 25/716, *sb. pl.* seats

Seiȝtnesse, 82/570, *sb.* reconciliation

Seik, 22/628, *vb.* seek, look for

Seimit, 28/813, *vb. pt. t.* seemed

Seir, 3/25, *adj.* different

Selcouthly, 24/680, *adv.* curiously, strangely

Semblay, 14/359, *sb.* assembly, meeting

Semelie, 17/461, *adv.* becomingly

Sen, 4/51, *conj.* since, as

Senȝeorabill, 25/717, *adj.* lordly, seignorial

Seriaunce, 48/413, *sb.* *pl.* soldiers: those who served. Lat. *servientem*, acc. of *serviens*, pr. p. of *servio* = to serve

Seruit, 9/183, *pp.* served

Sesit, 32/926, *pp.* invested with

Set, 23/637, *vb. pr. t.* reckon, consider

Sey, 106/1393, *vb. pt. t.* tell

Sib, 31/901, *adj.* related

Sic, 4/33, *adv.* so, such

Sikinge, 96/1063, *pr. p.* sighing

Sindrie, 4/29, *adv.* in different directions; 10/223, *adj.* sundry, various

Sir, 9/202, *adv.* frequent, many

Sit, 6/99, *vb.* disregard, disobey

Skaith, 28/824, *sb.* hurt, injury

Skill, 4/57, *sb.* reason, sense

Slane, 31/900, *pp.* slain

Sobernes, 19/527, *sb.* quietness, peace

Solempnit, 15/406, *adj.* solemn, sacred

Soudanis, 31/901, *sb. pl.* sultans

Souerance, 30/883, *sb.* mercy, sufferance

Spaird, 23/656, *vb. pt. t.* questioned, enquired of

Speid, 16/428, *vb.* speed, hasten

Speir, 4/53, *vb. pr. t.* ask, enquire

Speris, 4/51, *vb. pr. t.* askest

Sperpellit, 3/26, *vb. pt. t.* were dispersed

Splenders, 28/814, *sb. pl.* splinters

Sprent, 28/815, *vb. pt. t.* sprang, leaped

Springis, 31/904, *sb.* spring

Spuilȝe, 31/904, *vb.* spoil, ruin

Squechonis, 24/686, *sb. pl.* escutcheons

Squyary, 11/275, *sb.* attendants

Stad, 22/605, *pp.* bested, pressed

Stakkerit, 8/153, *vb. pt. t.* staggered

Staluartlie, 4/32, *adv.* bravely, courageously

Start, 31/895, *sb.* a moment, a brief space

Stede, 102/1279, *sb.* place

Steek, 114/1661, *vb. pt. t.* barred

Steill, 17/474, *sb.* steel; 22/606, *vb.* steal

Steir, 16/413, *sb.* stir: on steir = astir, moving

Steird, 8/175, *pp.* stirred, aroused

Steiris, 3/12, *vb. pr. t.* hastens, starts

Steuen, 59/815, *sb.* a voice

Stonischit, 8/175, *pp.* astounded, astonished

Stound, 22/622, *sb.* moment, minute

Stour, 30/868, *sb.* fight, contest

Straid, 4/32, *vb. pt. t.* moved, struggled

Straik, 8/175, *sb.* blow, stroke; 28/815, *vb. pt. t.* struck, smote

Strait, 26/734, *adj.* narrow

Stray, 18/479: ? on stray = astride

Stubill, 19/522, *adj.* little, sturdy

Stude, 17/456, *vb. pt. t.* stood

Sture, 3/16, *adj.* rough, strong

Stynt, 25/702, *vb.* stop

Succuderus, 31/912, *adj.* arrogant, presumptuous

Succudiously, 30/859, *adv.* arrogantly, haughtily

Suddand, 20/542, *adj.* unexpected, unforeseen

Suith, 4/52, *sb.* truth, sooth

Summoundis, 6/99, *sb. pl.* orders

Suppois, 11/259, *vb. pr. t.* am sure, warrant

Swayne, 22/609, *sb.* man

Swere, 52/549, *sb.* the neck

Swoir, 32/945, *vb. pt. t.* swore, took an oath

Swyith, 6/116, *adv.* quickly, at once

Syne, 6/185, *adv.* then, afterwards

Syȝ, 87/738, 745, *vb. pt. t.* saw

Ta, 21/568, *sb.* take

Taillis, 10/223, *sb. pl.* tales, stories

Tak, 32/941, *vb.* surrender, give up

Takin, 17/459, *sb.* token, sign

Tane, 30/889, the tane = one : for that ane = that one; 8/158, *pp.* received

Targing, 89/833, *sb.* tarrying, delay

Teind, 18/476, *sb.* tithe, tenth part

Teir, 18/476, *adj.* tiresome

Tene, 7/123, *sb.* anger

Tenefull, 17/460, *adj.* awful

Tent, 13/316, *sb.* notice, attention

Teuch, 19/523, *adj.* tough, strong

Thairin, 4/28, *adv.* therein, in it

Thairun, 14/376, *adv.* thereon, on that

Tharth, 20/538, *vb. impers.* ought, it behoves

Thay, 3/2, *art.* those

Thocht, 8/166, though, although; 8/178, *vb. pt. t.* seemed, appeared good to him

Thopas, 18/470, *sb.* topaz stones

Þorte, 68/104, *vb. pt. s.* ought. A.S. *þearf*

Thourtour, 21/569, *adj.* cross, transverse

Thra, 28/804, *sb.* eagerness, speed in thra = eagerly, speedily

Thraly, 23/659, *adv.* eagerly

Þratten, 87/736, *v. pt. pl.* threatened

Thrawin, 7/129, *adj.* out of temper

Threip, 5/79, *vb.* quarrel, fall out ; 9/199, *vb. pr. t.* declare constantly

Threttie, 14/345, *num. adj.* thirty

Threttis, 23/659, *sb. pl.* threats

Thrife, 4/53, *vb.* thrive, prosper

Thring, 9/199, *vb.* thrust, shoot

Thristit, 23/659, *vb. pt. t.* thrust himself, pushed

Throw, 25/699, *adv.* eagerly

Thus-gait, 8/171, *adv.* thus, in this manner

Ticht, 17/459, *pp.* tied

Til, 112/1619, *conj.* while

Tine, 106/1397, *vb.* lose

Tit, 16/434, *vb.* drag

Tite, 45/294, *adv.* soon : *also tite* = at once

To-blaisterit, 4/28, *vb. pt. t.* blew furiously

To-come, 94/996, *sb.* coming, arrival

To-drof, 113/1646, *v. pt. s.* hew in pieces

To-morne, 5/85, *adv.* to-morrow

To-queiȝte, 98/1114, *v. pt. s.* shook

To-worne, 20/562, *pp.* worn to pieces

Towsill, 16/434, *vb.* use or handle roughly

Traist, 4/55, *vb. imp.* trust, believe; 20/548, *adj.* trusting, confident

Trauale, 4/48, *sb.* work, labour

Trauellouris, 5/82, *sb. pl.* travellers

Trew lufe, 18/475, ? true-love knots

Trimland, 17/460, *pr. p.* trembling

Trist, 101/1221, *adj.* confident, bold

Tuggill, 19/523, *vb.* struggle, strive

Tuik, 3/25, *vb. pt. t.* took, followed

Turnit, 3/4, *vb. pt. t.* returned, started back from

Trow, 30/880, *vb.* believe

Tyne, 4/58, *vb.* to be lost, to perish; 28/827, to lose

Tyt, 7/123, *vb. pt. t.* took, seized

Tyte, 30/876, *adv.* quickly, at once

Tything, 21/584, *sb.* tidings, report

Vmbekest, 16/412, *vb. pt. t.* looked round, cast his eyes round

Vnburely, 19/524, *adj.* rough

Vncourtes, 7/122, *adj.* uncourteous

Vndeid, 29/858, *adj.* alive, unkilled

Vnderfenge, 39/87, *v. pt. s.* received

Vnderta, 10/243, *vb. pr. t.* engage, promise

Vnder-ʒat, 105/1351, *v. pt. s.* understood

Vneis, 8/157, *adv.* scarcely

Vngane, 23/663, *pp.* not yet gone

Vnkend, 11/249, *adj.* unknown

Vnknawne, 7/127, *adj.* ignorant

Vnrufe, 4/47, *sb.* trouble, toil

Vnsemand, 7/148, *adj.* improper, unseemly

Vther, 3/3, *adj.* other

Venov, 60/845, *sb.* an encounter

Veseir, 29/842, *sb.* vizor

Vincussing, 29/828, *vb.* vanquishing, conquering

Wa, 11/249, *adj.* unwilling, sorry

Wachis, 11/276, *sb. pl.* watchmen, guards

Waird, 27/763, *sb.* fate, destiny, chance

Wait, 4/46, *vb. pr. t.* know

Wald, 15/407, *sb.* moor, downs, wolds

Walkand, 5/73, *pr. p.* travelling, walking

Walkin, 11/277, *vb.* awake

Walkinnit, 12/282, *vb. pt. t.* woke up, awoke

Wan, 17/462, *vb. pt. t.* won, gained

Wandit, 14/360, *vb. pt. t.* wound round, tied

Wane, 3/7, *sb.* palace, dwelling

Wantoun, 6/100, *adj.* free, quick. O.E. *wantowen* = ill-educated, from *wan*—prefix, signifying *want*, and A.S. *togen*, educated, *pp.* of *teón*

Wapnis, 29/838; wappinis, 19/517, *sb. pl.* weapons, arms

Wardecors, 106/1409, *sb.* a bodyguard: hence, an attendant, a squire

Wardroparis, 11/276, *sb. pl.* keepers of the wardrobe

Warysoun, 31/919, *sb.* reward

Waryþede, 101/1231, *v. pt. s.* ? cursed or was annoyed

Wassalage, 30/890, *vb.* action becoming a knight, a great achievement

Wayndit, 10/230, *vb. pt. t.* cared, liked

Wedderis, 3/21, *sb. pl.* weather, storm

Weidis, 20/562, *sb. pl.* clothes

Weild, 32/926, *sb.* enjoy, possess

Weildit, 21/580, *vb. pt. t.* ruled, was master of

Weill, 4/46, *adv.* well

Weir, 12/290, 25/706, *sb.* doubt; 10/230, hesitation

Weird, 15/379, *sb.* fate, destiny

Weit, 6/106, *adj.* wet

Wem, 57/745, *sb.* a stain. Compare *Sir Ferumbras*, l. 5725

Weryouris, 27/769, *sb. pl.* warriors, fighting men

Weschin, 7/145, *pp.* washed

Wicht, 4/36, *adj.* rough, boisterous ; 27/792, valiant, doughty

Wickit, 3/20, *adj.* boisterous, tempestuous

Widdeis, 14/368, *sb. pl.* ropes made of twigs of willow

Will, 4/35, *adj.* lost, astray

Willar, 7/140, *adj.* more lost, astray

Win, 6/110, *vb.* succeed ; 22/627, *vb.* find out, seek ; 32/928, *sb.* pleasure, enjoyment

Winnis, 19/529, *vb. pr. t.* dwells, lives

Wirk, 32/932, *vb.* work, act

Wise, 16/436, *adj.* in one's senses, sane

Wist, 3/21, *vb. pt. t.* knew

Wit, 95/1032, *sb.* blame ; 10/228, *vb.* know, be informed

With thy, 5/70, provided, if

Witten, 22/606, *pp.* known

Wold, 101/1228, *sb.* power, rule. So in *Sir Ferumbras*, l. 334 ; and *Perceval*, 2006 :
    "That had those londis in *wolde*."

Wond, 46/340, *vb.* turn, move

Worschip, 28/827, *sb.* prize, glory

Worthis, 24/694, *vb. pr. t.* has become, there is

Worthyest, 9/188, *adj.* finest, best

Wosche, 10/217, *vb. pt. t.* washed

Wox, 4/35, *vb. pt. t.* became, was

Wraith, 6/100, *adj.* angry, wrath

Wrake, 38/40, *sb.* destruction

Wreche, 105/1364, *sb.* ruin, calamity

Wrocht, 11/266, *pp.* made, prepared

Wroþerhele, 51/532, *sb.* an ill fate, ruin

Wy, 21/580, *sb.* men, nobles

Wylit, 25/712, *pp.* beguiled, seduced

Wyn, 31/921, ? pleasant

Wynning, 10/229, *sb.* dwelling, residence : thy maist wynning = thy usual residence

Wythest, 27/769, *adj.* most valiant, mightiest

Yare, 39/83, *adv.* ready

Y-corn, 49/448, *pp.* chosen

Y-schent, 51/508, *pp.* disgraced

Ȝaf, 71/192, *pt. s.* gave (a thought)

Ȝaip, 22/630, *adj.* crafty, cunning

Ȝair, 22/643, *adv.* earnestly, carefully

Ȝald, 10/226, *vb. pt. t.* gave, returned

Ȝarne, 29/840, *vb. imper.* think, consider

Ȝed, 20/547 ; Ȝeid, 7/131, *vb. pt. t.* went, proceeded

Ȝeir, 9/202, *vb.* year

Ȝeman, 22/630, *sb.* servant, attendant

Ȝern, 44/275, *adv.* readily, easily

Ȝerne, 23/643, *sb.* take care of

Ȝet, 22/611, *vb.* ; Ȝettis, 23/635, *sb. pl.* gate, entrance

Ȝilte, 94/978, *imp. sb.* yield

Ȝole, 49/442, *sb.* yule-tide : Christmas

Ȝone, 25/708, *adv.* yonder

Ȝule tyde, 3/4, *sb.* Christmas

For Product Safety Concerns and Information please contact our EU
representative GPSR@taylorandfrancis.com
Taylor & Francis Verlag GmbH, Kaufingerstraße 24, 80331 München, Germany

www.ingramcontent.com/pod-product-compliance
Lightning Source LLC
Chambersburg PA
CBHW071419300726
48976CB00004B/1175